*For my mother-in-law, Hiromi*

*GreatFindHotelBookings.com*

*L'Hotel Bouchard is a delightful boutique hotel situated within the famous quarter of Saint-Germain-des-Prés. The mid-priced, family-owned hotel combines comfort with sophistication. A five-star experience at a three-star price.*

*Comfortable beds and crisp linens, and modern amenities, such as a hair dryer and air conditioning, mean this stylish hotel will revive even the weariest traveller. Start each day with a delicious continental breakfast before exploring the city. Conveniently located close to all the top tourist sites, the hotel is the perfect Paris base. If you're looking for a Paris hotel that combines classic architecture with understated elegance, look no further than the magnificent L'Hotel Bouchard.*

*Nearby: The Louvre, the Musée d'Orsay, the Jardin des Tuileries.*

*Book here.*

JANE TARA

## THE LOST GIRL SERIES

#1 Fish Out Of Water

#2 Off The Map

#3 #RealLife

#4 Excess Baggage

#5 Passport to Freedom

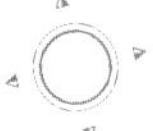

First Published 2019 by
Redback Publishing
PO Box 357 Frenchs Forest NSW 2086
Australia

www.redbackpublishing.com.au
email: orders@redbackpublishing.com.au



ISBN: 978-1-925860-45-0

Author: Jane Tara
Edited by April Sieczkowski
Illustrations by Jenya Bes

A catalogue record for this book is available from the National Library of Australia

# CHAPTER One

This could not be it.

Hana stared at the crumbling building, speechless.

This couldn't be the hotel she'd spent four months trawling the Internet to find. Not the place she'd eventually settled on, knowing with absolute certainty that it would be the perfect place for her and her four best friends to stay when they arrived in Paris, her dream city, where only a dream hotel would suffice.

What was this monstrosity before them now? This definitely wasn't the hotel she'd booked.

Four of the five girls stared at the hotel in silence. Beautiful, blonde Ada huddled up to Dina, as much for comfort as warmth against the cold. Dina pulled a beanie out of her bag and yanked it down over her long brown locks, until it covered her ears. Frankie seemed the least concerned and took some shots of herself blowing icy fog out of her mouth. Meanwhile, Mae bowed her head as she scrolled through her phone. Her pink hair shone in the early morning light, and her Chelsea boots tapped on the sidewalk as she moved her legs to keep warm.

"This is definitely it," said Mae.

The girls left their bags in a pile and huddled around Mae's phone.

"That's some serious airbrushing. It's like the Kardashian of hotels," Dina quipped.

Hana still refused to believe what was now obvious. "The website said it was opposite a small park."

All five girls turned their heads in unison to see the park across the street.

"Is that man urinating on the swing set?" Ada asked, the pitch of her voice rising in horror.

Hana snatched the phone off Mae and once again fell for the delightful little hotel advertised online, with its charming facade and newly refurbished interior. She'd been in charge of organising the Paris leg of their trip and refused to stay in a hostel. Hana had been waiting her whole life to visit Paris. She wanted to do it properly. Again checking the address, Hana looked back at the street around them. They were definitely in the right place. The wrought iron sills and marble steps leading into the foyer certainly weren't as shiny as they were in the photos. This ramshackle building must be the most photogenic hotel on the planet. The difference between the photos and the reality was astounding.

"You've got to be kidding me." Hana was close to tears. She noticed Frankie taking a photo of her. "I'll never speak to you again if you put this on Instagram."

Frankie threw her head back and laughed. Nothing fazed her. She'd grown up being "worldschooled", travelling with her parents. She rolled with the punches, so to her this was nothing but a very minor hiccup. "Hey, I've got to make a living, and this is gold."

"It's not gold. It's really upsetting to me."

Frankie shrugged. "My family once arrived at a hotel we'd booked only to find it had been demolished."

"That would have been better than this," Hana snarled.

"We should go inside." Dump or not, Ada sounded relieved that they'd found their hotel. She was outside her comfort zone every step of the way on this trip. The act of travelling wasn't easy for her. "I bet it's lovely inside."

"I'll sue them for false advertising if not," Hana said.

Dina hauled her bag towards the entrance. "C'mon, it's cold and I need to pee."

"Just use the swing set," Hana snapped, lifting her bag off the pavement. "This monstrosity is hurting my eyes."

"Then shut them," Dina laughed.

Hana shut her mouth instead. She was furious. But still, Ada might be right. The website had shown stylish rooms with refurbished antique furniture and a view across the sixth arrondissement. It had some great reviews and was reasonably priced.

As much as she could afford to stay somewhere more expensive, she was mindful of the fact that her friends couldn't. Apart from Frankie, who was making a mint from her Instagram account. But Ada, Mae and Dina had their budgets and Hana was sticking to one too, but that didn't mean her dreams of a stylish Paris hotel were going to be squashed. She'd spent countless hours searching online to find the right hotel. Something chic but within budget. And L'Hotel Bouchard was meant to be it. There wasn't a great deal about it online, but Hana had seen that as a plus. It wouldn't be overrun by tourists. Because while she was fully aware that she was a tourist herself, that didn't mean she wanted to be around any others. Hana was here to fulfil a dream: Paris. And this hotel was meant to be the foundation for that.

She followed her friends into the foyer, paused, and gave the place one sweeping, melodramatic look. The others watched her, clearly taking cues from her reaction.

It was dark, with faded drapes and furnishings and the smell of damp dog. The height of the ceiling, the ornate light fittings and balustrades suggested a time of glory, but now it felt sad and claustrophobic.

"What a dump."

"The rooms still might be better," Dina reasoned.

"Yeah, and I might be Marie Antoinette."

"Perhaps in a past life." Frankie rang the bell on the front desk. "C'mon, let's check in and if it's really bad, we can look for something else when we go out today."

The girls all waited silently.

Frankie hit the bell again.

Finally, a tap, shuffle-tap sound in the distance.

Tap-shuffle-tap.

Tap-shuffle-tap.

Until a door swung open and in walked an old woman with a walking stick. She smiled at the girls, clearly delighted to see them.

"Bonjour, Mademoiselles."

"Bonjour, Madame. J'ai une réservation sous Hana Honda. I asked for an early check-in."

"Oui," the woman said. "From Australia."

Hana watched the elderly woman carefully. She was small. Probably a head shorter than herself and Hana was only five foot four. But her presence was much larger. She was wearing a Chanel suit, which Hana picked for early seventies. Slightly worn around the cuffs, but otherwise in mint condition. Pearl earrings, black hair with one long streak of white, all pulled into a tight bun. The slash of red across her lips bled into her wrinkles and her nose looked powdered. She had neat manicured nails, and her weathered fingers were decorated with two rings on each hand, all gold and huge sapphires.

"Is this your family hotel?" Hana asked.

"Oui. I am Bouchard. It 'as been in my family since 1723. My grandfather made ze conversion from townhouse to 'otel."

"It's a little different to how it's depicted on TripAdvice."

"We 'ave both seen better days."

Hana bit her tongue. It was true, they had, but both the hotel and owner must've once been something else. It was barely eight in the morning and the woman was wearing stockings. There was a fresh bouquet of flowers on the desk behind her. Hana felt guilt wash over her. Yes, they'd both seen better days, but they were both still trying. Okay, the hotel didn't fit with the image she had in her head, but that was no reason to be rude.

Madame Bouchard slid two room keys across the desk and smiled at the girls. Her teeth were smeared with lipstick.

"Third floor. Ze elevator is broken so please use ze stairs."

Hana pasted a tight smile across her face. "Thank you."

And, with that, Madame Bouchard turned and tap-shuffled her way through the door and out the back.

"What, no porter?" Hana sighed.

Mae picked up her bag and started hoiking it up the stairs. She clearly wasn't feeling jet-lagged. Dina and then Frankie followed, while Ada struggled with her bags behind them. Ada thought travel light was something you read with on a night flight. Hana made her way behind. She felt so brutally disappointed that she could barely lift her legs.

"Sorry, Ada," Hana apologised. "It looked completely different online."

"It's not your fault, sweetie." Ada puffed. "Besides, I'm having fun."

Hana was grateful for the lie. She knew Ada had been on-edge since she'd had a panic attack in Tokyo. She'd pulled herself together with some help from Mae, who she trusted implicitly with her 'issues', and decided to continue with their long-planned, post-HSC adventure. But Ada was still clearly a little shaky. Even so, watching Ada deal with this drama now made Hana realise just how far her friend had come since they'd left Australia two weeks ago. And she didn't just mean geographically. Ada was facing her fears head-on, and Hana was impressed. Ada was made of stronger stuff than she gave herself credit for.

Hana hauled her bag to the top of the stairs and checked for the room number, counting doors down the long, dim hall as she passed them.

"This is like something from The Shining," she said. "Remember that movie?"

"How could I forget? It scarred me for life," Ada said.

"It scarred us all," Frankie said. "Lucky we had each other."

They came to their doors. Ada, Mae and Frankie disappeared through one, and Hana watched Dina put the key into theirs. As they entered, Hana prayed to the gods that the room was better than what they'd seen so far.

The gods were busy.

Or royally pissed off.

They certainly weren't listening to her.

The supposedly spacious twin deluxe suite was actually a pokey dogbox, perfect for torturing claustrophobics. The small double bed (where were the twins she'd booked?) had a sagging mattress and the carpet was frayed and stained. It was worse than disappointing. It was depressing.

"It really did look different online," Hana said weakly.

"Hey, stop saying that will you? It's pretty hideous but it's not like you designed the place." Dina knew that Hana planned to be an interior designer. It's why this leg of the trip was so important to her.

Hana believed Paris was the design capital of the world. From fashion to furniture, Paris was the leader. Hana had been waiting to come here her whole life and she wasn't going to let a little setback like a dodgy hotel ruin it.

Dina seemed to read her mind. "We can go out and get a bite to eat and check out some other hotels on the way. There's no problem moving elsewhere. If that's what you want. Do you want to find another hotel?"

Hana looked as if she'd just been handed a winning Lotto ticket. "God yes, give me one good reason to stay here."

And with that, the bathroom door swung open and out walked a guy wrapped in nothing but a towel. Tall, black hair, shoulders you could land a plane on.

Hana and Dina screamed. While the hot guy certainly seemed surprised to see them, he didn't run for cover, or yell at them. Instead he grinned.

"And I thought this hotel had no room service."

# CHAPTER Two

Hana looked at Madame Bouchard in despair.

"Are you telling me your hotel—this hotel—is completely full?"

"Oui."

Hana was ready to admit defeat. "Then we'll need a full refund and we'll go somewhere else."

"Zat will be very difficult."

Hana gave her a cold stare. "I'm sure you can arrange a refund."

"Of course I can refund, but it will be very difficult to find another room in Paris zis week."

"What do you mean it will be difficult finding a room in Paris this week?"

"Ze Pope is visiting. Many tourists are 'ere to see ze Pope."

"The Pope." Hana stared at Madame Bouchard with a look of utter disbelief.

"Our first stop in Europe should've been Rome," Dina said. "It'll be quiet there."

"There must be one empty room in this city," Hana said, her voice rising.

Madame Bouchard was calm. "Mademoiselle, if zis hotel is fully booked, zen all 'otels in Paris are fully booked."

Hana took a deep breath. Clearly Madame Bouchard knew her hotel was every tourist's last resort. Paris's Last Resort. Hana almost sniggered at her new name for the Bouchard. Le

Last Resort!

"Madame Bouchard." A deep voice echoed through the foyer.

Hana turned to see the guy from her room, now fully dressed and striding towards the front desk. He spoke to Madame Bouchard in rapid-fire French, too fast for Hana's limited language skills to completely follow. She was only able to pick up that it was something about another room.

Madame Bouchard gave a nod and then shuffled over to a display of keys and removed one. Returning to the girls, she pushed the key across the desk with a resigned smile. "Zer is one room that slipped my mind."

Dina took the keys and turned to thank the mystery guy, but he was already heading back up the stairs.

Who was he?

Was he a family member? Did he work at the hotel? Was he a regular guest?

Hana asked Madame Bouchard. "That guy—gentleman. Is he a staff member?"

"He is 'andsome, no?"

That threw Hana. "Not really my question."

Madame Bouchard shrugged. "Is there anything else, Mademoiselle?"

"Er, no, that's all."

Hana and Dina headed for the stairs. "A bit bloody evasive. He might be an axe murderer and she sent us into his room."

"That would explain his ripped arms. All that swinging a heavy axe… builds muscles," Dina chuckled.

Hana looked at her friend as if she was missing the point. "You don't think it's creepy that he appeared out of the bathroom, then disappeared, and suddenly reappeared downstairs to find us another room? It's weird."

"He was as surprised to see us as we were him. And we were the ones who screamed and disappeared. He just followed us after he put clothes on. A tragedy up there with the end of Game of Thrones."

It was true. Hana couldn't help but take a good hard look at him while she backed out of the room. Male physiques like that didn't come along very often. So she'd absorbed the muscular arms and ripped six-pack and then stormed reception, demanding an apology. Instead, Madame Bouchard gave her a sly smile, as if she didn't see what the problem was.

Hana had to admit; she had been rather melodramatic. They'd never been in any danger. That was clear from the way he'd smiled at them, embarrassed but friendly. Then tried to placate them as they backed out of the room.

"Well, let's hope there are no more naked surprises in our new room," Hana said, rather unconvincingly.

Keys in hand, Dina and Hana returned to the floor where they'd left their luggage and made their way along the corridor to their new room. Hana was so exhausted now she almost didn't care what it looked like. Almost. Upon opening the door, both girls paused on the threshold.

"Is this the same hotel?" Dina said as they entered the room.

Their new suite was stylish, with soft colours, lots of light and elegant furnishing. Everything was spotless and yet still retained an old-world charm.

"Finally," Hana whispered.

"This is the room featured on the website," Dina pointed out. "It's as if just one room has been renovated."

Hana placed her bag on the luggage rack and unzipped it. "You know you should never put your belongings onto a hotel bed until you've checked for bedbugs?"

Dina rolled her eyes. "Okay, you check for bedbugs while I message Ronin and tell him we're here." Dina grabbed her iPad and disappeared out the door to find the Wi-Fi password.

Hana was going to have to get used to Dina dating her older brother, Ronin. It had been an interesting couple of weeks in Tokyo, getting to know Dina and watching her and Ronin fall for each other.

Dina was Mae's sister. She hadn't been at school with the rest of the group. In fact, she'd done her HSC a year earlier at a school for elite athletes. Her whole life had revolved around being a swimmer. So even though Hana, Ada and Frankie had met Dina before they'd left Australia, they didn't really know her. In Hana's mind, Dina had been Mae's seriously impressive older sister, and never around.

Dina had been roped into the trip because Mae was too young to travel alone. Mae was… unique. Her brain worked in a way that Hana often found difficult to grasp.

She was younger than her friends since she had jumped ahead a couple of school grades. Mostly, it wasn't obvious, but there were regular reminders of the age gap.

Like two years ago, when one-by-one, they all got their driver's licence, but Mae had only recently got her L plates. And when the four friends decided to go travelling after they finished school, but the only way Mae's parents would allow her to join them was if Mae had a guardian go with her. That person was her older sister, Dina.

Hana was thrilled to have Dina along now, but it had been a bumpy start. Initially, Dina didn't want to be there with them. She'd been through a rough time personally, and the last thing she needed was to go travelling with her sister's friends. Dina had been training for the Olympics, but a guy with a grudge derailed those plans when he spiked Dina's drink so that she tested positive to a banned substance after a race. Dina was left high and dry, out of the pool, and on a plane to Tokyo.

Of course, travel has a way of changing people. It's never just about external geography. There is always an internal journey as well. And Dina's included falling for Japan… and for Hana's brother, Ronin, who lived in Tokyo.

Hana was pleased for them. She really liked Dina. She had guts. And Hana adored her brother, even if he had been difficult in Tokyo. Hana had issues with Ronin during her stay, including one argument that still hurt and was left open. He'd arrived at the airport unexpectedly, not wanting her to leave while there was still tension between them. But Hana knew how stubborn her brother was. The big reason he showed up was to talk with Dina. He was there to save his relationship with her, not fix things with his sister. They were close, extremely close, but Hana understood more than anyone how complex her argument with her brother was, and how they alone would have to resolve it by taking action on something that was too painful to fathom. Certainly too painful for Paris. She needed to put it aside, for later.

Hana stripped and stepped into the shower. The bathroom was lovely, with granite finishes and a spacious shower. She needed to clear her head so she could enjoy Paris.

The water ran in rivers down her body, washing away the stress of arriving in Paris, the argument with Ronin, and everything that had led up to it.

# CHAPTER Three

"I'm home." Hana swung the screen door open and marched into the house. She dropped her school bag near the staircase and wandered into the kitchen. "Ma'aarm?" She drew the word out and let it echo around the house. "You here?"

Her mother was always somewhere around when she got home from school. She worked part-time at Hi Ho but had the luxury of working hours that fitted around her children.

Hana opened the fridge and stared at the contents until it beeped, reminding her to close the door. She grabbed the cheese and pulled the sandwich maker from the cupboard.

That's when she heard her parent's voices upstairs.

Muffled, angry voices.

She didn't move, listening to see if she'd misheard. Her parents never argued.

Her mother's voice became shrill, bouncing off the walls above Hana's head. Hana stared up at the ceiling as if she'd see her parents there. Then her father's voice, pleading and—was he crying? Had someone died?

Hana turned and legged it for the stairs. As her foot hit the first step, there was an all-mighty smash from her parent's room. Hana mounted the stairs two at a time and burst through the door just as something hurtled towards her. She screamed and ducked and something smashed against the wall beside her.

Standing again, she took in the scene before her. Her mother was still in her pyjamas. Her blonde hair was all over the place, as if she'd styled it in a blender. Her blue eyes were swollen and wild. Her pale skin blotchy. It was clear she'd been crying for hours.

Her father was still wearing his wetsuit from his morning surf, yanked down so he was naked from the waist up. His left shoulder was covered in a carp tattoo, dedicated to the wife who was crying before him. It took her parents a moment to realise that Hana had entered the room. They both froze. Despite their obvious fury, they still glanced at each other as if asking the other what they should do.

"What's going on?" Hana screamed.

"I'd like to know the same thing," said a voice from behind.

Hana turned to see Ronin. She threw herself into his embrace, away from the unfamiliar madness between her parents.

"Mum, Dad, what's happened?" Ronin asked.

Hana expected her parents to calmly explain what was going on. She also knew there would be a good explanation. That's how things worked in their home. Instead, her mother's head rolled back and she let out a terrifying howl.

"Your father is having an affair."

Hana felt the floor drop from beneath her.

Ringing in her ears.

A blurry film covering the scene before her.

It all seemed distant.

The only thing she was certain of was the grip Ronin had on her. His fingers pressed into her shoulder.

Ronin's voice was steady. "Dad, is this true?"

Their father looked at them, his eyes filled with pain and remorse. "It is. It is and I'm so sorry."

Their mother crumpled to a heap on the floor, quietly crying now, into the crook of her arm. Hana extracted herself from

Ronin and ran to her mother, holding her on the floor.

"It's nothing," their father continued. "It means nothing."

"Then why would you do it?" Ronin bellowed.

Hana watched her brother glare daggers at his father. And then he turned and disappeared down the stairs. The front door banged a moment later.

"Ronin," Hana screamed after him. "Don't leave me here."

But he was gone, his car screeching down the street.

Her father took a step towards her, as if he wanted to comfort her, but Hana shook her head. "No, Daddy… you should go."

And so he left too.

***

The shower water washed away the tears. She knew she was being silly, dwelling on that day. But it was the day things had changed.

She soaped her hair with her L'Occitane shampoo and began to rinse when the water turned icy cold.

"Oh damn!"

Hana grabbed at the taps and wiggled them around. She turned the cold off completely, waiting for the hot water to return. It didn't. The water was freezing and she still had a head full of shampoo.

"Double damn."

Sticking her head under the water, Hana squealed as the temperature stole her breath. She quickly rinsed the shampoo out and slammed the tap off. Forget conditioner, she didn't have the pain threshold. She was freezing now.

Wrapping a towel around her head, she quickly dressed,

"Bad news," Dina called, coming back into the room.

"I know, there's no hot water."

"No Internet either."

"What do you mean? It's down?"

"No… it doesn't exist."

Hana quickly got dressed. "How can that be possible?"

"Madame Bouchard said…" Dina added a thick French accent. "… ze Internet is something I don't understand so I never bothered getting."

"I wonder if she'd feel the same about heart surgery if she needed that."

"She said if we want 'ze Internet'… to go elsewhere."

"She probably does it so no one can Google alternative accommodation while they're here."

Dina laughed. "She's a genius. Hey, don't look so upset. You're not going to cry, are you?"

Hana yanked the towel from her head and started rubbing her hair dry, along with her eyes. "Nope, all good."

"Remember what you told me on that first day in Tokyo?"

How could Hana forget? The girls were staying in her parent's Tokyo apartment and, when Hana organised the sleeping arrangements, she put Dina in the tatami room. Dina's initial relief at sleeping alone turned to anger when she saw that the room wasn't furnished. She didn't understand that it was Hana's favourite room, or that in Japan tatami was revered, so giving Dina that room was a show of respect. Dina didn't appreciate the cultural differences at first, but by the time she left Japan, she did.

"Yes, I remember when you bitched about the tatami room."

"I didn't want to be there. In that room, or in Japan. But now I wouldn't change a thing. As much as I despised it in the beginning, it changed my life. It taught me that sometimes things aren't as you expect them to be. So, how about you relax a little and let's find the great things about this place too."

"It's not what I imagined."

"Well, to be fair, I never imagined sleeping on the floor in an empty room at the time either." Dina said. She dragged Hana over to the window and pulled back the dusty curtain. "I bet we have a great view."

They stared out onto the building next door and straight into the living room of a middle-aged gentleman wandering around his apartment in boxer shorts, a big belly tumbling over the top.

"I told you we'd have a great view."

"That wasn't on the website either."

Hana looked at Dina in horror, but Dina was too busy laughing. After a moment, Hana joined in and the two girls doubled over, tears of laughter on their cheeks.

"Remind me to mention this in the TripAdvice review," Hana laughed.

"It can't get worse," Dina guffawed.

"Nope, we've hit peak awful." And that's when Hana realised that if you ignored what was directly opposite, and turned your attention to the right, the room actually had a lovely view. While not spectacular—no direct view of the Eiffel Tower or Notre Dame—it was Parisian. Rooftops, cobbled pavements, a woman walking a dog.

Dina followed Hana's gaze. "That's nice."

Hana nodded. "It's a start."

# CHAPTER Four

"So, this is where we do it?" Hana asked, taking in the café around her. She approved. Maybe the day was about to get better. "Good choice, Mae."

Mae stared at her phone. "Maybe not. No Internet. Hold on." She motioned to a waiter nearby. "Excusez-moi, do you have the Wi-Fi password?"

"We don't have customer Internet." He replied in perfect English.

"Do you know where does?"

His lip curled slightly. "Starbucks, Mademoiselle."

Frankie rolled her eyes. "Wish we'd known that before we ordered."

Mae turned back to her friends. "Change of plans. Breakfast at Les Deux Magots first, and then Starbucks for our results."

The others put their phones away.

Breakfast at Les Deux Magots was Mae's idea. The girls had agreed that their first morning in Paris had to include breakfast somewhere 'typically French'. They wanted the full carb hit of pastries and more pastries, and some caffeine on top, as they logged on and checked their HSC results.

It was a big moment, and Hana couldn't help but notice that it coincided with the first morning in the city of her future. She expected to have done well. They all did. Apart from Frankie, who really didn't care.

Not that any of them had been particularly focused on their

results until now. They'd been too busy enjoying Tokyo and life after school. In fact, the further away from school they got, the less important the exam marks seemed, despite the pressure they'd put on themselves at the time.

Especially Mae.

Mae had changed on the trip. The longer she spent away from home (and her controlling mother), the more outspoken she was about her intention to be a writer. That was not her mother's plan. Mae had a science scholarship to the University of Sydney, but right now that was the last thing on her mind. She was more interested in the literary history of their café.

"I know Les Deux Magots is now filled with tourists, but it has such an incredible literary history," Mae chatted, looking around the place as if she'd just arrived in heaven. Her pink hair stuck out from under a wool cap. "Simone de Beauvoir, Jean-Paul Sartre… All the literary greats would eat here. The literary expat set too. Hemingway, James Joyce, Brecht. There's even an annual literary prize named after the place." Mae slapped the table for emphasis. "Countless great writers sat here."

"Did they all check their HSC results here?" Ada asked.

"They would've… but no free Wi-Fi."

Les Deux Magots was quintessentially Parisian with its tables spilling out onto the sidewalk. The girls were settled into a table in the centre of it all, taking in the scene around them.

Mae continued with her history lesson. Hana didn't mind. Mae was smart and interesting, and usually shared information that was relevant. Today it was all about Paris, so Hana was happy to listen.

"You know, cafés have always been a meeting place for intellectuals in Paris. Even freedom fighters from the

French Revolution would meet in cafés to plan their attacks. Conversations in French cafés were important. It's so inspiring."

"How things have changed." Hana watched as Frankie took thirty selfies, chose one, edited it and then posted it to Instagram.

Frankie smiled at her. She was so relaxed and pretty with her lithe, long limbs and dark hair. "So, tell us more about the guy in the shower, Hana."

Dina laughed. "Hana went twenty shades of mortified."

Hana rolled her eyes. "FYI, I was actually summing up the situation and working out the best way to run if he attacked us."

"Do you usually blush under threat?"

"Yeah right, I wasn't blushing." She gave her friends a suggestive wink. "It was hot in the room."

The others laughed.

"Who do you think he is?" asked Ada.

Dina grinned. "Well I got a good look at him too, so my vote is for underwear model. Definitely an underwear model."

Hana laughed. "Maybe. And he's staying at the hotel while he's in Paris shooting a commercial for... Calvin Klein or something."

Mae swung her chair back onto two legs. "He's not a guest."

"What makes you think that?" Hana asked.

"You said he told Madame Bouchard to give you that room, you know, the renovated one that just slipped her mind. She held back on purpose, but clearly he pulled rank on her."

"Good point," Frankie said.

"Maybe he's a family member?" Dina said.

"Her son? Or grandson?" Ada said.

Hana shook her head. "No, he's not."

"How do you know?"

Hana played with her cutlery. "I can't pick where it's from, but his accent isn't French."

There was a collective intake of breath around the table.

Frankie gave her a look of faux horror. "Not French? You know what that means?"

"Yes. It means I'm not interested."

The girls all nodded. They understood.

Their order arrived and silence descended while they all tore into an array of brioche and croissants with jam and Poitou-Charentes butter, and a pain au chocolat each. The flaky pastry melted in Hana's mouth. She washed it down with a pot of hot chocolate, perfect against the cool outside temperatures.

"I could die and go to heaven," Ada murmured. She loved desserts and was the cook in the group, often baking treats for her friends. "Here, Mae, have a bite of this one."

Hana turned her attention to the street around her. She was determined to throw off her disappointment over the hotel and reconnect with why she was in Paris. From a very early age she had loved Parisian style and design. While her friends were reading Harry Potter, she was devouring books on French design houses and interior decorating. She knew more about the slight differences in Louis XVI, Louis XV, and Louis XIV chairs than she did about the Kardashians.

Hana had known from a young age that she wanted to be an interior designer. There was never any doubt. Her aim was to study design at university. She'd worked hard in high school and today was the day that it paid off, getting her marks, here in Paris.

The reason for this visit was to start immersing herself in the key features of Paris design. Haussmann-style apartments with their hardwood floors and elaborate ceiling mouldings. A fabulous chandelier and gilded mirrors. The juxtaposition of modern furnishings with antiques. Intricate elements, warm hues and sophisticated style.

Paris had always been Hana's dream. It was a big part of her life plan: to visit now, soak everything in, and work out how she could live in the city after graduating university. The hotel had been a disappointing start, but watching the world go by now was helping her forget that.

Mae had been looking at her phone but now spoke directly to Hana. "I've just put together a little walking tour if you're up for it. Or do you want to drop by some hotels?"

"What's the point while the Pope's in town?"

"Should we go and see the Pope?" Frankie joked.

"Good idea," Hana said. "And ask him to leave so we can move hotels."

Dina finished her coffee. "There's so much to see that we won't spend enough time at the hotel for you to notice how awful it is."

"It's a beautiful day," Ada said. "I could do with a long walk to clear my head."

Ada had devoured her pastries. That was a good sign. Ada never ate when she was anxious. The struggles she'd overcome while they were in Tokyo seemed to make her stronger.

Mae jiggled around in her seat. She was rarely still. "I've mapped the route. But first… let's get it out of the way."

The others nodded. They'd all agreed to eat first, check their marks, and then continue on with their day, even if they were disappointed.

Especially if they were disappointed.

CHAPTER

# Five

"Log in, check your results, and then provide us with a brief response. Are you happy or not? No jumping into the Seine."

Ada, Hana and Frankie all started tapping at their screens. Mae sat back and sipped on a frappuccino. "Not bad," she said. "Not as good as the hot chocolate at Les Deux Magots, but drinkable."

"What are you doing?" Dina asked.

"Reviewing my morning refreshments," Mae said.

"Aren't you going to check your marks?" Dina asked her sister.

Mae tugged at the cuff of her striped sweater. "Nope."

Hana's eyes drifted up and watched the exchange. Mae was gifted. Everyone expected her to blitz the HSC. She could very well top the state in some subjects.

And yet she showed zero interest in checking her results.

Was she for real?

She seemed to be.

"I might check once the ATARs come through. I'm not really interested today."

No one pushed her. She already had a full scholarship, so her marks were irrelevant.

"Okay, when you're ready." Dina was the only one not actually getting her results. She'd done her HSC the year before and, until a spiked orange juice derailed her swimming career, had been at university and training for the Olympics.

She knew a thing or two about bouncing back from disappointment.

The girls were huddled around a small table. Dina shared a bench chair with Hana.

"Shall we call Ronin after you check your results?" Dina asked her.

Hana felt a familiar tightness in her chest. She'd decided in the shower to just enjoy Paris and then resolve the argument with Ronin afterwards. When they were in Italy or somewhere not quite as important to her.

"You can," she said.

Dina sighed. "I wish you guys would tell me what this is all about."

"I'm sorry, I will, I promise. It's more timing than secrecy." That wasn't entirely true. Hana was a private person and had a habit of keeping things to herself. She wasn't like Frankie, who was comfortable sharing her whole life with the world. She wasn't even willing to share everything with her friends, and not because she didn't trust them.

"You'll work this out. You're so close. And, until you do, I'm not choosing sides. I'm here if you need a friend." Dina put her head down and started messaging Ronin.

There was an immediate ping back and Hana watched her friend's face light up as she started an exchange. She felt a tug of jealousy. Not over Dina and Ronin. She was really happy they were together. But she wondered when her time would come to fall in love.

She'd never even been close.

She'd never had a boyfriend. Never really had a crush on anyone. She'd liked one of the guys from her neighbourhood growing up, but one fumbling experience at a local Christmas party had turned her off. He'd been so focused on what he wanted from her, but not at all concerned about her feelings. And when she'd pushed him away and jumped off the lounge, his response had been, "What's your problem?"

It had taken some time for her to work out what her problem had been. Weeks of obsessing about the incident and wondering if there really was something wrong with her, as he'd suggested.

But finally she did work it out, and she realised there was nothing wrong with her. She wanted something special. Something intelligent. She wanted a boy who was a little old-fashioned, and willing to be patient and take time getting to know each other.

She wanted to be romanced.

And she wanted to be sure.

And if that made her a bit different, then so be it. There were billions of people on the planet. There must be one guy out there who was a match for that.

And surely one in Paris.

Hana thought about the hot guy from the hotel and then tried to dismiss the thought just as quickly. He was in Paris, but wasn't French.

Hana turned her attention to her own phone.

An apprehensive hush fell over the group while they took their time to absorb their results.

Frankie was the first to respond. "Okay. All good from me. I'm happy enough with that."

Ada followed, looking up from her phone with a smile. "Better than expected."

"That's because you worry about everything and totally underestimate your own intelligence," Mae teased.

Ada breathed a sigh of relief and slipped her phone into the pocket of her jacket. "You might be right."

Everyone's eyes rested on Hana. She could feel their gaze as she scanned her results. She checked that she'd logged into the correct account. That couldn't be right.

Her heart sank. Her marks weren't awful, but definitely not as good as she'd hoped. As she'd expected.

Her visual arts results were great, but everyone knew that didn't scale well. She was relying on Maths and English and really thought she'd done better than that in English. Now she was worried about her ATAR and admission into her first preference for university.

"Hana, how'd you go?" asked Dina.

She looked up at her friends and forced a smile. She wasn't ready to share her disappointment. "Good. All good," is all she could manage.

Mae jumped to her feet. "Thank god that's done. Let's hit Paris."

Hana followed her friends down the street, breathing in the cool air and the sights of the world's most famous city. But her mind was back in her school study hall, wondering how she'd messed up that essay question so badly.

# CHAPTER Six

The girls spent the rest of the day getting lost. Mae had mapped out a general route to take, but then put her phone away and they'd winged it from there. Taking wrong turns down medieval laneways, past cool coffee shops and boutiques, wandering through markets and poking through old bookshops. Everything was exciting. The food: cured meats, rich pâtés and stinky cheeses. They watched old men playing boules in a local square. Soaking up the tranquillity of Luxembourg Gardens, they then took photos at Shakespeare and Company and headed to Notre-Dame.

A sombre mood fell over the group as they took in the damage to the cathedral. While they couldn't get too close, they could clearly see the destruction where the spire used to be and even still make out all the cathedral's smaller details from the perimeter where they stood.

Mae was the first to speak. "From what I've read, the reason it didn't burn to the ground is because of its architecture. The Gothic style was developed to take over the Romanesque style, which was a higher fire risk. More wood I think. Anyway, Gothic cathedrals rarely catch fire."

"Thanks for that history lesson, Miss," Dina teased, giving her sister a light shove.

Mae giggled. "Want to play I Spy a Gargoyle?"

The others laughed and the mood lifted.

They made their way around viewing spots along the

perimeter spotting gargoyles, and grotesques. Mae called out to the others each time she spotted a new one. "See the open mouths? The gargoyles are waterspouts, to help drain rainfall from the cathedral. The statues also came in handy scaring the crap out of local parishioners. Keeping them scared of demons and hell kept them coming to church."

"You really know the weirdest things," Frankie laughed.

"That's why we love her," Ada said. "She fits in with the rest of us weirdos."

With her pink pixie cut and overalls, and her exuberant energy, Mae didn't present as your stereotypical genius. She didn't look like the kids in national spelling bees, or the ones you saw on the local news who'd just been accepted to study astrophysics at Harvard. She was a fascinating combination of over-excitabilities, over-sensitivities, and high intelligence. At times, she seemed like the old soul of the group, while at others she definitely showed her age. She had an eidetic memory but couldn't remember to wear socks. She was disorganised, forgetful and delightfully clown-like. Her giftedness didn't only present as the hardworking A-grade student. It presented in ways that frustrated her teachers, and mostly her mother.

With her friends, Mae could be herself. There was no judgement, just complete acceptance. If anything, the girls had all been drawn together because all of them were not only smart, but also outsiders.

Frankie had been homeschooled until she met the others on her first day in their real school. Her unusual upbringing had made it impossible for her to conform.

Ada's beauty drew everyone towards her, like moths to a flame. But she was never comfortable with the attention, and her anxiety was often misinterpreted as her being strange.

Hana had initially been courted by the cool girls at school who knew she was from a wealthy family. But Hana didn't like the same things the rest of her peers liked, and she came across as aloof.

Individually, each member of the group was unusual. Together, those wonderful and weird aspects of each personality blossomed.

"Time for Hana to get her geek on," Mae called over her shoulder.

They made a beeline for the Marché aux fleurs, the oldest flower market in Paris. The girls all knew how much Hana loved flowers. Learning ikebana from her Japanese grandmother had given her an appreciation of not only flowers, but the design elements used in a beautiful arrangement or bouquet.

She knew it wasn't what most people her age were into, so felt a surge of gratitude for her friends.

They loosened their scarves as they entered one of the pavilions, relieved to get out of the icy wind blowing off the Seine. The stalls were packed with winter shrubs and trees, hanging baskets and potted plants, but still the place was ablaze with colour. Hana breathed deeply, a symphony of scents greeting her. While spring was no doubt the most spectacular time to visit the market, there were still flowers and plants here that would be unavailable anywhere else.

Hana lingered by a stall of citrus trees in full bloom. The smell of the blooms and fruits seemed out of place in the Parisian winter. She ran her hand across some of the decorative pots that Parisians used to jazz up their balconies. She asked a stallholder what a couple of plants were, but the woman was abrasive and spoke in rapid French. Succulents, cacti, pomegranates perhaps.

She wandered on through the stalls of linens and pottery

and knick-knacks. Decorative birdcages and birdhouses swung above her head, waiting for each Sunday when the Marché aux fleurs became a bird market. Some stalls were doing a roaring trade in Christmas trees, festive wreaths and decorations. Hana took her time looking at how the florists had woven the berries and pinecones through the Christmas flower displays.

They made their way slowly through the market, before eventually emerging into the winter sun again. They backtracked and crossed the Pont Neuf (which Mae explained means 'New Bridge' even though it is the oldest standing bridge across the river) and wandered the embankments of the Seine.

"Is that the Louvre? Oh my god, is that the line to get in?" Dina said.

"We've booked a tour for early Monday morning," Mae said. "Remember, you complained."

"I take that back. Early is good. Let's get in and out before the crowds."

They passed Place de la Concorde and headed to the Champs-Élysées.

It was there Hana knew something was very wrong. She wasn't miserable. She wasn't even obsessing on her English results, although it was certainly on her mind. It's just she was in the street she'd dreamt about for as long as she could remember. It was meant to be the most beautiful shopping street in the world, filled with elegant boutiques and luxury brands. The wide streets, the expensive stores, the cafés and restaurants and the beautifully dressed women who strutted past them all. And it meant nothing to her. She felt completely disconnected, like she wasn't really there.

The whole avenue was adorned with Christmas lights, dripping from the trees, already alight now that the afternoon sun was starting to set.

The Arc de Triumphe stood tall at the end.

Mae skipped around her, pointing out different hotels that she knew Hana wanted to see. Hana pretended to be happy to be there.

The historic Hôtel de Crillon.

A detour to the exclusive Hôtel Champs Élysées Plaza in its Haussmann-styled mansion.

And finally, a turn down Avenue George V, and the one hotel Hana had asked to see the inside of months ago, when they were planning the trip: the Four Seasons Hotel George V.

It was a moment Hana had been looking forward to and sure of.

Just like checking her HSC results.

# CHAPTER Seven

Hana and her grandmother were placing some flowers in a vase. Unlike most people, who fill the vase with water and plunk the flowers in it, they had separated the bunch and were now choosing each flower, stem by stem and deciding where it should go.

"I am happy your parents named you Hana," she'd said. "Ronin, what is that? It's not a real Japanese name. But Hana is a beautiful name."

"It means flower," Hana said.

Baba nodded. "Yes, flower. But much more. You understand, tsuki ni muragumo, hana ni arashi?"

"I think. Clouds over the moon, storm over blossoms?"

"Life can bring trouble even in the happiest of times."

Hana gave her grandmother a quick hug, to change the subject. "That's a bit depressing, Baba."

"Not depressing. Just life."

***

Hana stood in the lobby of the George V and thought about her grandmother. Flowers always reminded Hana of her grandmother. Their love of flowers and design had been a deep, shared bond. She wanted to visit the George V in honour of her grandmother. But now that she was here, she realised her grandmother would have hated it.

She would have thought the whole scene was over-the-top. It was a jaw dropping display of flowers. Not only were there a number of spectacular floral arrangements, but there were also a few huge sculptures and installations made out of lights. And in the centre of it all was a huge, bejewelled Christmas tree. The girls walked over to the window where they could see more trees lit up in a courtyard.

"Every week, twelve thousand flowers are brought here from Amsterdam," Hana explained to the others.

Mae's eyes widened. "It's unbelievable."

"Over the holiday season they don't use as many flowers, so they add the extra decorative things like lights and candles."

Frankie was snapping away. "These will look unreal on Insta. Are they just in the lobby?"

"There are nearly two hundred displays all over the hotel. But the main public areas have the major ones." Hana said. "The florist is famous. Jeff Leatham. He's like the rockstar of flowers. Every three weeks, he and his team develop a floral theme for the hotel. Obviously this one is influenced by Christmas."

"This is possibly the most beautiful place I've ever seen," Mae sighed.

"It's magical," said Ada.

There was no doubt it was incredible, thought Hana, but she could almost sense the spirit of her grandmother beside her, sighing as she would when she saw something she deemed too extravagant. Her grandmother expressed beauty through simplicity.

Hana was extremely fortunate that her parents had provided her with the opportunity to cut her design teeth on a couple of projects. She'd completely overhauled her grandparent's beachside home in Japan after they'd passed away, and also done the interior of Ronin's small Tokyo apartment. Both places had been influenced heavily by her Japanese heritage.

She'd always had a picture of Paris in her mind, including the floral arrangements that were now before her. And while it was everything she expected, she wasn't feeling moved by it. It was beautiful, but it didn't hold a candle to her grandmother's ikebana arrangements.

Suddenly, Hana felt incredibly Japanese. Of all the places to experience such a moment! Why didn't she feel that sense of connection when she was actually in Japan? Hana had never felt overly Japanese, but then she'd also never truly felt Australian. She was both, and yet neither.

She hugged each of her friends and pretended to be thrilled they'd taken her to the hotel. She didn't mention the internal war that was waging.

They made their way back outside and towards the Seine again, crossing at Pont de l'Alma and towards the final destination on their walking tour: the Eiffel Tower, rising up in the distance.

The crowds around them began to thicken. A large Chinese tour group loitered around one area. The girls made their way around the group, laughing with each other, chatting, stopping to take photos. Excitement was in the air… this was the ultimate Parisian moment.

And then there it was. Right there. Touching distance.

Hana stared up at the Eiffel Tower. After all the years of dreaming and reading everything she could get her hands on about Paris, she was actually here.

And she was totally and utterly shocked to feel… nothing.

Okay, nothing was an exaggeration. She simply didn't feel what she thought she'd feel. She'd always imagined a sense of coming home.

Perhaps some elation.

Joy.

She'd experienced none of that today, despite enjoying herself.

She wasn't having an awful time.

She just didn't have the time she'd expected.

Hana tried to work out how she felt. Everywhere they'd gone, it felt familiar. It was exactly how she'd imagined it to be and more. A never-ending expanse of beautiful buildings, amazing sights. She'd enjoyed every step of the long walk to end up at the Eiffel Tower. And yet, none of it was a surprise. None of it moved her. None of it made her feel at home. None of it was what she expected. Scrap that. It was exactly what she expected, it just wasn't how she expected to feel about it.

Had their hotel stuffed up her whole trip?

No, she was more resilient than that. It was just one hotel in a city that was meant to be her spiritual homeland.

What the hell was going on?

Her HSC marks? Maybe. She was definitely disappointed.

And she was jet-lagged. Yes, that was it. Perhaps all the things she expected to feel would come tomorrow.

Frankie waved all the girls over to grab some photos. She really was getting more obsessed with the selfies, but Hana tried not to judge. After all, Frankie's Instagram account paid for her trip. This was her job.

Hana joined in the photos, not wanting to be a downer, and gave some big, fake smiles. But inside she was in turmoil, trying to understand why she wasn't more excited to be in Paris.

Why she didn't feel anything.

She smiled along with her friends, staring up at the symbol of Paris, but inside a surge of anger began to build. She quickly went from numb to furious. Why did she feel like this? Rage built. Suddenly, on the inside, Hana was screaming. The feeling intensified in her chest until she could hear the scream ringing around her.

Screaming!

But it wasn't her. It was Ada.

# CHAPTER Eight

"Stop! Help me!"

Tourists scattered around them.

A woman was grabbing at Ada. They were grabbing at each other, with Ada trying to get away from the other woman's grip.

Dina and Mae rushed forward and started pulling Ada towards them. The woman shoved Mae aside, but Mae returned with a swift kick to the woman's shins. Dina lurched at the woman, pushing her away from her sister and friend. The strap to Ada's bag snapped and the woman finally ran in the opposite direction.

"She stole my bag!" Ada was hysterical.

Ada's bag was swinging from the woman's arm as she pushed through the crowd. Hana almost chased after her but knew that was foolish, so instead scanned the area for a police officer. She spotted one in the distance. "Help. Au secours! Help!" she shouted, waving her arms.

The police officer turned and began running towards them. Hana searched the crowd again for the thief but there was no sign of her now. She'd disappeared.

Ada was sobbing in Dina's arms.

Mae was trying to gauge if Ada was hurt.

And Frankie had her phone out, having taken photos of it all.

"Put your phone away or I'll smash it," Hana screamed.

Frankie looked like she'd been slapped. "I took a photo of the thief."

Hana felt chastened but didn't speak.

Frankie turned away from her.

The police officer reached them and spoke rapid French but quickly changed to English when he realised that's what the girls spoke.

"Can you provide a description?" he asked.

Frankie took her phone from her pocket and showed him the photos she'd taken. He nodded, as if he understood the situation clearly. "I am afraid your 'andbag is gone. We can make a report, but you must cancel everything, such as credit cards and passports."

Hana felt the ground below her sink. More drama in Paris. Now they would be wasting their time at a local police station. That bag was never coming back.

"What did you have in the bag?" Hana asked. If only Ada would stop crying. She was clearly headed for one of her meltdowns. More people gathered around them. Where were they when the girls needed help? Everyone was watching now, both fascinated and horrified by the state of the stunning young woman.

"Ada, what was in your bag," Hana snapped.

Ada stalled enough to speak. "There was nothing in my bag."

The police officer looked as confused as Hana felt until Ada unzipped her jacket and lifted her jumper and shirt slightly to show a security pack strapped around her slim waist.

"I have everything here. I just had a small change purse and some makeup in my bag."

"Why carry a bag then?" Hana asked.

Ada started sobbing again. "I'd read about thieves in Paris, so carried it as a dummy bag."

Mae lifted her layers. "She made me wear one too."

Hana laughed. She had to. If she'd seen that an hour earlier, she'd have dismissed it as Ada being overly anxious. But now it saved them hours dealing with banks and embassies. She pulled her own small bag around to the front of her body and kept her arm across it.

The police officer spent a few more minutes checking that there was indeed nothing of value in the bag, and that Ada wasn't hurt in the robbery. He was clearly concerned about her, given her howling. And there didn't seem to be an end in sight with that.

"Where are you staying?" he asked Hana.

Hana told him the address of the hotel. It was no surprise he'd never heard of it. He insisted that he call a nearby police van to drive them back there.

Hana really didn't want to get into a police car. "She'll be fine in a minute," she said to the others.

Mae shook her head.

"I think we should get her back to the hotel as quickly as possible," Dina said.

The others agreed and the police officer made a call. Within minutes, a white van with blue and red stripes down the side and 'police' emblazoned along it had pulled up nearby. The police officer led the girls over to it.

"I 'ope you enjoy the rest of your time in Paris," he said.

The other girls thanked him for his help, while Hana just stared at him as if he were mad.

The doors closed and moments later they were speeding off, into the traffic.

Hana watched the Paris streets fly by. They passed two West African women with colourful headdresses, a stylish Middle Eastern woman in a Chanel jacket and hijab, some tourists and hip students, and two old women who had stopped to talk to each other. She spotted another black woman wearing her hair in an elaborate up-do. That was style. She noticed a couple of Japanese women, easy to spot in their immaculate designer clothes. She lowered her head further, immediately feeling ridiculous.

The irony wasn't lost on her that in her first few hours in her spiritual homeland of France, that she felt more Japanese than ever. And, being Japanese, she was utterly humiliated to be now sitting in a police van. She was meant to be soaking up all there was to learn about Paris, at the Cité de l'architecture et du patrimoine, or the Cité de la mode et du design, or the Musée des arts décoratifs at the Louvre. Hell, she was happy to rewind to Starbucks. Anything but sitting in a police van, anywhere in the world, let alone in Paris.

She reached into her bag and grabbed her sunglasses and beanie and shoved both of them on her head.

"I don't think anyone here knows you," Frankie snapped.

"I'm just being careful, in case you take a photo of this for Instagram," Hana retorted.

Frankie turned away and Hana slid down in her seat, hoping the trip would end soon.

***

Hana stood at the window, her fingers lightly touching the wooden shutters. Theirs was not the type of home that had the police visit. Their beachside home was luxurious and open plan, an oasis of calm for the close-knit family. It was a home usually filled with laughter, family games nights and a lot of love. For three weeks now it had been quiet, apart from her mother's crying. Shutters were pulled low, marring the ocean views. Hana had juggled school and study, along with household chores and cooking dinner for her and her mother. Not that either of them ate much.

Hana watched her parents now, standing by the police car. They'd been forced into each other's company again. Someone had stolen a series of designs at Hi Ho, for a new board that her father had designed. He'd been talking about it for months; certain it was going to change surfing.

As angry and hurt as Hana was, she knew what the designs meant to her father. To the family business. The police were involved and just today the case had blown wide open. The thief had sold the plans to a number of competitors. This led to his arrest.

And to him being driven home in the police car.

Ronin stepped out of the car and onto the curb. He looked dishevelled and tired.

Hana watched as their mother pulled him into her arms. Ronin looked like he was crying. And then she stepped back, and Ronin stood before their father, his head hanging. He looked ashamed.

Their father turned to the police officer and shook her hand. Then, gently, he wrapped an arm around his son and led him back into the house.

***

They'd pulled up in front of their hotel. Ada's crying had settled.

"Here we are," said Mae.

Ada was actually pulling herself out of her meltdown.

She was breathing deeply, eyes closed, in the way she'd been taught to calm herself, counting in and then out. They all sat and watched her for a moment. And then she opened her eyes and looked at her friends, and to everyone's surprise, quietly said, "Don't say I never take you anywhere."

CHAPTER

# Nine

Dinner was an awkward affair at a Chinese noodle restaurant near their hotel. It was cheap and close and none of the girls were up to wandering the streets in search of the perfect place to eat.

To Hana, a Chinese noodle bar was the perfect place to eat. It was so opposed to how she'd expected to spend her first dinner in Paris that it was the perfectly awful topping on a perfectly awful day.

"What a hell day," Dina said. She placed her hand on top of Ada's. "How are you doing?"

Hana noticed that Ada hadn't touched her food, which was always a sign that she was struggling. Most people would take one look at Ada and simply think that she was blessed. So it was usually assumed that life for Ada was easy. It wasn't. Ada had Obsessive Compulsive Disorder and, with that, anxiety. Incidents like today were big for anyone, but for Ada they were mammoth. The girls were all aware of the signs that came with Ada struggling. One was when her anxiety amped up, making it difficult for her to eat. The stress of unexpected events sent her mind into a loop. The result was she wouldn't eat when they were out. It wasn't just a lack of appetite but also when her mind obsessed over the food being contaminated. She simply couldn't eat food she hadn't prepared herself.

Frankie took one of Ada's spring rolls from her plate. "No point wasting it," she said as she shoved it in her mouth.

"Ada might still eat that," Hana snapped.

Frankie didn't respond. She still wasn't talking to Hana after the photo incident earlier.

"It's fine," Ada said to Hana. "I'm not hungry. I'll admit today has sent me into a spin, which is why I'm not touching my food."

The girls all stared at Ada in surprise. They were used to addressing Ada's issues by talking around them.

They said things like, "Ada's feeling a bit stressed at the moment".

Or "Ada's friend is hanging around today", meaning her OCD.

All language they'd learnt from Ada's mother.

This was new; Ada confronting it head on.

"So, you might as well know I'm looping a bit," Ada said, referring to what happens in her brain. A look of defiance settled across her beautiful face. "But I don't want you to worry about me. I'm handling it."

Mae was Ada's great protector. Had been from the moment they met. She clapped her hands together. "Because you gave a big eff you to that thief. Your greatest fear about Paris was being robbed. Remember we spoke about it? So, you came up with the dummy handbag idea, which I went along with."

"You said it was a genius idea," Ada said.

"I lied. I thought it was overkill."

"You did?"

Mae shrugged. "Turns out you were right, and your plan was the perfect solution."

Ada smiled. "I do keep thinking about her searching my bag for valuables and coming up with nothing but some euro coins and a Woolworths Rewards card."

"Not to mention the snack bars." Mae explained to the others. "Ada figured that if someone was desperate enough to steal her bag, that they might be hungry. So she put snack bars in her dummy bag."

Frankie slapped the table. "I love it. That's so you. I wish I had a photo of that."

Hana rolled her eyes, but Frankie noticed.

"Did you just roll your eyes at me?"

"I've got something in my eye," Hana lied.

"I know you're judging me, but I don't have a rich father paying my bills."

"I get that," Hana snapped. "I just think your timing is off with some of the photos."

"I wasn't taking an Instagram photo today. I actually photographed the thief."

Hana didn't apologise. She wasn't sure Frankie was telling the truth. And, even if Frankie was, Hana wasn't in the mood to apologise. She was angry: with Frankie, with the thief, with the hotel, with Paris.

To make matters worse, the sexy guy from the hotel had been leaving the hotel as the police van dropped them back. Hana actually saw him do a double take as they all piled out onto the pavement.

Embarrassed didn't come close to how she felt.

Hana pushed her chair back and grabbed her bag. "I'm going back to the dog box."

She left the restaurant, willing herself to not cry. She didn't cry very often. She bottled everything in. Ronin said it made her more Japanese than she realised, locking her feelings away, so others weren't witness to them.

Hana was stressed about her ATAR. It was hitting her hard

now. She really hoped it was high enough but had her doubts now. There was no plan B. The next few years had been mapped out, but nothing seemed to be going to plan.

She knew she was angry, and perhaps she was unfairly taking that out on Frankie. But she couldn't shake the feeling that she didn't trust her anymore.

Hana spotted a McDonald's and made her way across the road, where she stood outside and logged onto their Internet. She opened her rarely used Instagram. She occasionally posted a photo of a design element or piece of furniture that she wanted to remember. She searched for Frankie's account.

412000 followers.

Wow, she really had built that up.

Hana scrolled through the photos. Frankie took great photos. She really had an eye for it. Being incredibly photogenic also helped. It was easy to see why she was popular. With her big smile and free-flowing hair, people were drawn to her. She looked healthy and happy and like she was embracing life.

All truths, Hana had to admit. Frankie did embrace life.

Hana looked for the photo from today, but it wasn't there. She felt a surge of guilt. Frankie did just take that photo of the thief to help catch her. She hadn't posted anything.

But then she noticed another photo further down. She clicked on it and stared at it for a moment, her stomach in knots.

This was worse. Way worse.

Dina caught up to her. "Hey, we'll start again tomorrow. Not every day can be great. We're bound to have a few bad ones."

"I know," Hana said, shoving her phone away. "I'm just disappointed it happened to be the first day in Paris."

"It's over and done with now. Tomorrow we're going to paint this town gilded gold. Deal?"

Despite herself, Hana smiled. "Deal."

Dina paused for a minute. "Do you want more food?"

"No, why?"

"You're outside McDonald's."

"I was using the Wi-Fi to check my messages. C'mon, let's go." Hana headed towards the hotel. She couldn't wait to see the end of the day. Tomorrow would surely be better. She steeled herself as they entered the hotel. There really was a bad odour to the place. She ignored the smell and the peeling paint and the worn carpet and headed straight for the stairs. The girls didn't speak until they were in their room.

"I don't want to be as paranoid as Ada, but where's your passport?" Dina asked as she locked the door behind them.

"In my carry-on," Hana said.

"Get it out. Get all your valuables. I've been really slack with mine, leaving things lying around, but I think we should get into the habit of knowing where those things are."

Hana nodded. "True. We'll be staying in hostels in Italy, so that's probably smart."

They both rifled through their bags, grabbing their wallets, passports and backup credit cards. Then they put everything into one bag.

Hana washed her face and cleaned her teeth, and then joined Dina in the double bed.

"One day we'll laugh about today," Dina whispered in the dark.

"I'm sure we will," Hana admitted. "When we're old and sitting in a nursing home together."

Dina giggled. "You know the really great thing about that?"

"What?"

"It means we'll still be friends."

Hana hugged her pillow tight, glad she was there with Dina. As she drifted to sleep, like a mantra she kept telling herself: things can only get better.

Her father always reminded her when she was hurting, "Everything passes. This too will pass." He even sometimes said it when she was happy. "Everything passes. This too will pass." He wasn't being a downer… just Buddhist. And a realist… everything did pass.

He was right. This argument with Frankie would pass. But Hana felt that things would get worse before they got better.

# CHAPTER Ten

"FIRE!"

Hana sat upright, unsure for a moment where she was or what was making that awful trilling noise. Still mostly asleep, it took her a moment to realise Dina was standing over her, holding a jumper in one hand.

"Hana, up, now! The fire alarm," Dina screamed.

Hana shot up. The walls vibrated with the sound of the alarm, but there was something else hanging in the air, making her nostrils twitch.

"Is that smoke?"

Dina's panicked eyes said it all.

Hana leapt out of bed. "Get some proper shoes on, grab a coat and let's get the others." She was in full commando mode. She threw a jumper over her pyjamas and a jacket over everything. She tugged on her boots, grabbed her iPad and the pack that held both their passports and money. Thank god they'd put all of that in one bag earlier.

She tucked it under her clothes and headed for the door. The second she touched the doorknob she knew they were in trouble.

Her hand jolted away. "It's hot."

"What does that mean?" Dina asked.

"I think it means there's a fire right outside."

Dina ran to the window. "It's too high to climb out."

Hana took a deep breath. Don't panic. "Pull one of those wool blankets from the bed and wrap it around yourself. Wool is flame resistant."

Dina did as she was told, while Hana wrapped one around herself too.

Dina looked frightened now. "Maybe we should just stay here."

"And wait for what? A knight on a shining stallion to save us? This dump is on fire and if we want to survive we need to get out now."

Dina drew a deep breath. "You're right. We need to make sure the others are okay. I need to get Mae—" Dina's voice broke. She didn't need to say more. Mae was her world. Hana knew that.

The two girls looked at each other, wrapped in their wool blankets, as if they were wearing superhero capes.

"We can do this," Dina said.

Dina's eyes were wide but determined. "Damn right we can."

Hana flung the door open. Smoke billowed into the room, but then settled. She stuck her head around the door. The smoke was coming from the opposite end of the hall to the exit. "Stay low, under the smoke. We can breathe better down low."

"Where did you learn all of this?"

"YouTube."

Dina took a deep breath, as if she were diving into a pool and then, half crouching, she sprinted. Hana followed. There was a strange noise above them. The building creaked. They got to Mae, Ada and Frankie's room in seconds, yet it felt a lot longer.

Hana pounded on the door. "Open up! There's a fire."

Nothing.

She knocked again. "Wake up!"

Nothing.

"Maybe they've already been evacuated?" Hana said.

"Without getting us? No way."

"You're right." Hana pounded the door.

Something at the other end of the corridor exploded. Both girls screamed.

"Open the fucking door!"

"I'll kick the door down," Hana yelled.

A deep voice interrupted. "I think a key will be quicker."

Both girls spun around to find the hot guy behind them holding a bulky set of keys. He looked stressed, but in control. He moved in front of them and put a key into the lock.

"Why do you have a key?" Hana gave him an accusing stare.

"No time to be all judgy about that," Dina pointed out.

"It's the master key for cleaning," he assured her.

"Or when the hotel is burning down." Dina's voice was shrill.

"Yes, it comes in handy for such moments." He said as he opened the door.

The girls pushed past him to find their three friends sound asleep. Mae and Ada in the double bed, and Frankie in the single.

"Wake up, now!"

At the sound of Hana's voice, all three girls woke with a scream. Mae and Frankie pulled earplugs out and it was clear from Ada's disorientation that she'd taken something to help her sleep. No wonder they didn't wake.

Dina grabbed jackets and boots for her friends while Hana rallied them from their beds.

"The hotel is on fire. We need to get out now."

The hot guy stepped back outside the door and called to someone in French. The fire brigade had arrived. Out of the corner of her eye she saw him point to the direction of the fire and give instructions. He was pretty commanding. Who the hell could he be?

The hot guy (Hana thought she should probably stop thinking about him as the hot guy, considering how heated things actually were) turned back to her and they locked eyes. She suddenly felt hotter than the flames at the end of the hall. Hot guy was definitely the right name for him for now.

"Are you okay?"

"Of course," she said defiantly. "And I was perfectly able to save everyone without you magically appearing with that key."

"I don't doubt that for a second," he said grinning. "But we need to go now. If you want to get me out of here, that would be much appreciated."

She nodded and turned back to the others. "Make sure you've got your passports and let's go."

Mae scurried round the room grabbing everything, and then taking shell-shocked Ada's arm. Frankie followed Hana and Dina's lead and pulled wool blankets from the beds.

Hana could see the firefighters now, at the other end of the hall, their hoses aimed into one particular room.

Dina grabbed Mae's arm and pulled her out of the room. The others followed.

They were almost at the top of the stairwell when Hana realised that Frankie wasn't with them. She turned back and saw her friend a few metres behind them, pausing to take a photo up the hall.

"Frankie, get your arse down these stairs now."

Frankie didn't argue. She also remained silent as she bolted past Hana.

Ada looked petrified. Hana took the blanket from her own shoulders and threw it around her friend. And then, taking Ada's hand, led her and the others down the stairs. The foyer was filled with firefighters, who ran towards them, grabbing at them and escorting them outside. Judging from the size of the crowd on the pavement, they were likely the last guests to evacuate.

Hana did a headcount of her friends. She'd never forgive herself if something happened to one of them at the hotel she'd insisted on booking. Even Frankie, who had just put herself and Hana at risk over a stupid photo.

Dina and Mae were clutching at each other. Mae turned to Ada and drew her into their hug. Ada allowed herself to be held as she cried. This day had clearly been too much for her.

Hana turned to find Frankie, looking calm and taking another selfie in front of the burning hotel and frightened hotel guests.

Something stirred as she watched her friend. Hana turned away from her, disgusted.

And then she remembered the hot guy. She searched for him, to thank him for getting them all safely out of harm's way. And to apologise for seeming ungrateful that he'd shown up with keys. She knew that had saved them precious time opening the door. She just hated the idea of being saved by the guy… although turning up with a key certainly wasn't as gung-ho as kicking the door down. He hadn't tried to act like a hero.

She scanned the crowd. Her stomach twisted into a thousand knots.

They'd made it outside safely, but he was nowhere to be seen.

CHAPTER

# Eleven

Hana sat shivering in a blanket. An hour had passed and she was still outside. She was so cold that the fire inside the hotel was rather appealing right now. Anything to get warm. She could almost feel her tears turning into icicles the moment they fell to her cheek. Her teeth chattered and she once again looked around for the hot guy.

She'd already asked one firefighter about him when she'd realised that he hadn't made it out of the hotel with them. She'd blushed when she had tried to describe him, without giving away her nickname for him.

"Tall, dark hair," she'd said. "He helped us leave the hotel but I haven't seen him since."

The firefighter had shrugged. "We are doing everything we can."

There was nothing to do but wait. And freeze.

This complete shamble was not how she'd imagined Paris. Where was her Paris? She'd spent years dreaming about being in Paris. She'd spent months planning this leg of her trip. What happened to destiny?

Perhaps destiny didn't come easily.

Perhaps destiny challenged you.

Hopefully destiny got the hot guy safely out of the hotel.

She clutched the blanket tighter.

"Did you imagine Paris like this?"

Hana swung around; her relief obvious.

"I thought something had happened to you."

He seemed delighted by her reaction. "Were you worried about me?"

Hana stumbled over her words, embarrassed. "No… I mean… it was very kind of you to help us with that key, so I hoped you were safe too."

"I thought you were offended by me having a key?" He was enjoying teasing her.

"I apologise for that. Obviously, it was helpful."

"It was quicker, but I'm sure you were capable of kicking the door down."

"That was my plan." Hana grinned. It wasn't that cold anymore.

"I'm sure you didn't expect this when you decided to come to Paris."

Hana sighed, suddenly exhausted. "You have no idea."

"Your journey has gone off its map."

"Off what map?"

"When you travel, you have a map, even in here." He tapped the side of his head with one finger. "It's how you expect your trip to look. But I guess you didn't expect this."

"Oh no, I really hoped for a fire in the hotel. Always fun."

He laughed, which surprised her.

Hana locked eyes with the guy she now felt she knew exceptionally well. After all, he'd saved her life and she'd seen him nearly naked.

"I don't know your name," she said.

"I'm Drago."

You've got to be kidding me, Hana thought, even his name was completely wrong. Drago? What sort of name was that? Russian? Vampirish? Definitely not French. Why couldn't he be

Pierre, or Jean-Paul? Or at least ugly. Why did the hottest guy she'd ever met, who had just saved their lives, and was nice every time they met, have a name like Drago?

"I'm Hana," she said, before bursting into tears.

Drago put his arms around her and comforted her as if it were the most natural thing in the world. "Hey, it's okay. You're safe."

"It's not that… I know I'm safe. It's just, Paris sucks!"

"Tonight sucks, but that doesn't mean Paris sucks."

They drew apart while she explained herself.

"You don't understand. I've been looking forward to visiting Paris for years. My whole life. But the whole trip so far has been a debacle. The hotel looks nothing like it does on the booking site."

"Yes, it has been exaggerated."

Hana charged on. "And the Pope is in town so there are no other hotels. And then I got shit marks in English, which I thought I was going to blitz…"

Drago clearly had no idea what she was talking about but calmly listened.

"And the flowers at George V were a bit OTT if you ask me, and nothing I saw today moved me or inspired me, and then we were at the Eiffel Tower and Ada was mugged, so the police drove us home."

"Ah, so that's why—"

"Oh yes, and you saw me getting out of a police van."

"It certainly added to your mystery."

"Mystery? What did you think? That I'd been caught shoplifting, or robbing a bank?"

Drago shrugged. "I wasn't sure. Espionage perhaps? Something cool. Rather like how you come across."

Hana really didn't even need the blanket around her now, the heat that coursed through her body was so strong. "There was nothing cool about it. Never in my life did I ever expect to see the inside of a police van, let alone in Paris."

"Consider it an adventure," Drago said.

"It's not an adventure. It's humiliating. Top that off with an argument I'm having with one of my friends and—oh, let's not forget the hotel burnt down."

"It didn't actually burn down. The second floor has had considerable damage, and there has been some smoke damage in the foyer, but I can assure you, it's fine."

Hana glared at him.

"But I understand what you mean," he added. "More drama you didn't need on what has clearly been a stressful day." Drago's dark eyes ran across her face as if drinking her in. "Hana, it's okay. You can tell everyone all about this for years."

"I don't want to tell people about this. I want to tell them about the galleries and the great food and the fabulous hotel I stayed in."

"That's a boring story. Everyone does that in Paris. This is a good story."

"I don't want a good story. I want a good hotel."

"A good hotel is that important to you?"

Hana locked eyes with him, completely serious. "A good hotel, good design, is everything to me. I know that sounds ridiculous to most people my age."

His eyes peered deep into hers. "It doesn't sound ridiculous to me."

Her shoulders sagged. He really seemed to understand. "I'm just so disappointed."

"If it's a hotel you want, I know a good hotel you can stay at."

"I doubt it. The Pope's in town."

Drago clearly had no idea what she was talking about.

"The Pope is in Paris, so all the hotels are booked out," Hana explained.

Drago smiled, the type of smile that belonged on a cinema screen.

"Then this is your lucky day. My hotel is in Slovenia."

CHAPTER

# Twelve

All five girls were seated on fraying sofas in the foyer. The fire was out and the foyer was considered safe. The fire began with a small gas burner one of the guests had brought with them to cook their meals in their room. Although there had been a lot of smoke, the actual fire had remained contained to one room on the floor where the girls were sleeping.

The hotel guests had the option to find their own accommodation, or board a complimentary bus headed to a hotel an hour out of the city.

Hana watched one couple leg it out the front doors. "I don't know where they think they're staying."

"Maybe they're friends with the Pope," Ada said quietly.

"So, let me get this straight," Mae was grilling Drago. "You own a hotel in Slovenia and have asked us to stay?"

"That is correct. Although when I say I have a hotel, I don't mean me, personally. My family owns the hotel." Drago beamed at them all.

"His family owns a hotel," Dina said, deadpan.

"I don't know where Slovenia is." Ada's voice trembled.

"It's a small country bordered by Austria, Italy, Hungary and Croatia," Mae said. "It was a part of the former Yugoslavia."

"Geography doesn't really help me," Ada snapped.

"Slovenia is a beautiful country and very safe," Drago said. "It's part of the EU so you won't even need to change currency."

Hana looked at him. Was he lulling them into a false sense

of security? He seemed to understand that Ada needed to feel secure.

Frankie stretched her legs out and propped them on an ottoman. "It's true. It's a great country, and really lovely people. I was there with my parents a few years ago. It's one of their favourite places."

Drago's face lit up. "You've been to Slovenia?"

"We were in Ljubljana for a few days. And then we went to Koper and Piran for a week before travelling south along the coast, through Croatia."

"You haven't been to Lake Bled?"

"No. I saw photos and my parents said they'd love to go there next time."

"Then you must come, and we can visit Bled." Drago clearly thought he was offering them the chance of a lifetime.

Frankie seemed to agree. "Let's do it. Let's go to Slovenia."

"It's not part of the itinerary," Ada said.

"So?"

"I don't know anything about Slovenia." Ada's emphasis on Slovenia made it sound like she was saying 'I don't know anything about the Depths of Hell'.

Dina placed her arm around Ada. Their friendship had been forged in Tokyo and now she was as protective of Ada as her sister Mae was. "You've been coping so well here in Paris and we've been ripped off, mugged and evacuated a hotel because of a fire. I think you're underestimating what you can handle."

Perhaps Ada hadn't considered all that. Her mouth set in a determined grin. "You're right. Slovenia can't be worse than Paris."

"But it's not Paris," Hana snapped.

Drago shrugged. "Paris is not what you expected. Perhaps

this thing you are looking for is somewhere else?"

Hana glared at him. "Or it might be here in Paris tomorrow."

"Perhaps you should travel off your map."

"I'm not sure this saying of yours is translating properly, but that's not even the correct English, and I certainly don't have a map."

"Sounds like you have a very specific map of how Paris must look."

Hana clenched her fists. He was really annoying her. Especially the way he smiled at her now, a lock of his wavy dark hair falling over one eye.

Drago pushed his hair back and waved at more guests who were leaving. He turned back to the girls. "This hotel will now shut down tomorrow. Fire inspectors need to check the hotel, and then it will be renovated. The hotel has scoured the city for any available rooms, guesthouses and hostels. Most guests are being bussed to a hotel on the outskirts of the city tonight. You can join them… And in three days, once the Pope has left, you can find new accommodation."

"Bloody Pope," Hana mumbled.

"Or, you can be my guests at my family's hotel."

"In Slovenia." Hana sniffed.

Mae gave Hana a friendly slap. "Lighten up. I think Slovenia is a great idea. It's good for all of us. Frankie gets to see Lake Bled. Ada gets to challenge her itinerary. You get to go off your map…"

Everyone but Hana laughed. "What does Dina get?"

"I got everything I wanted or needed in Tokyo," Dina said. "From now on, I'm happy with whatever we do."

Hana clearly wasn't impressed by Dina's lack of support. She turned to Mae. "What about you?"

Mae gave Hana an angelic smile. "This turn of events makes for a better story."

Drago clapped his hands together in a large, joyous gesture. "Mae understands! You need a better story about Paris. Everyone visits the Louvre. Everyone eats croissants and camembert or roquefort. But you got mugged and escaped a fire and then had an offer to go to Slovenia. It's a much better read."

"That's true," Mae said.

"Reading is subjective." What if he were lying? They had no idea who he really was. "If your family own a hotel why are you staying in this dump?"

Drago looked sheepish. "Ah yes, that must seem strange."

Hana's eyes narrowed. Dina often said she'd be great working for the CIA, so now she was using that gift to nail him down and get the truth. "Surely a hotelier would stay in a proper hotel?"

"I normally stay at the Le Bristol when I'm in Paris."

Yeah right, thought Hana. The Le Bristol was an eighteenth-century mansion that had been turned into a luxury boutique hotel. Hana had virtually salivated over the interiors. She'd poured over the hotel's website, knowing she could hit her father up for the money to stay there, but the others could never afford it. It was one of Paris's most expensive, and certainly most beautiful, hotels.

"Right," Hana said sarcastically. "You normally stay at the Le Bristol?"

"That's correct. But this trip I had to stay here."

"Don't tell me. Because of the Pope?" Hana asked.

"Er, no… because… my father just bought it."

# CHAPTER Thirteen

The girls huddled around a table at McDonald's, which was Hana's worst nightmare in any city, let alone in Paris. But Drago had to deal with plans to close the hotel, and they needed to regroup somewhere and make a decision about his offer. McDonald's was close to the hotel, had Internet, and was the only place that was open.

Frankie ordered and passed the meals out while Mae googled "Drago Slovenia Hotels".

"Are they called French fries in France?" Dina quipped.

"They are known as Petite Frites," Frankie said. "See, Hana, McDonald's isn't so bad. It's still French. See le menu…"

"It's still le spew," Hana said.

Dina slugged back some cola. "How long is this 'poor me' routine going to last?"

Hana shot her a look. Dina had become her greatest ally, so the question stung. "How long did yours last?"

"About four months, but I can remember you were sick of it after about four hours."

Hana couldn't help but crack a smile. "You were a pain in the bum."

"I was. And then you took the baton and won't stop running with it."

Hana rested her chin on her hands. "I am tired. And not very sporty."

"Would it be so bad to head to Slovenia?"

Hana didn't answer.

Ada passed her fries to Mae. She was too wound up to be hungry. "I've felt a lot better since Dina reminded me what we've been through since arriving in Paris. I didn't have time to panic about all the dramas as they happened because we were too busy dealing with them. But I'd still like to make a decision tonight about what we'll do. Stay in Paris or take Drago up on his offer. And I have to sleep…"

She didn't need to finish the sentence. The others knew Ada needed her sleep to maintain her 'balance' as she called it. Ada was managing her fears well. She'd been tested in Paris, and although she'd had a meltdown after being mugged, she didn't actually have a panic attack. Those were frightening. For the first time in her life, she wasn't relying on her mother to make her feel safe. She was searching for ways to do that for herself. Every day was outside her comfort zone, and, while she wasn't entirely at ease yet, she also wasn't always on edge. She had her moments, but there were also moments where she let go. Where the thoughts inside her head didn't weigh her down. Moments where she was present and felt alive and, dare she say it, free.

Dina took the reins. It was hard to believe that just a couple of weeks ago she barely knew the other girls. "I know we had this whole part of the trip planned, or at least you had it planned, Hana. And we were all as excited as you. But things have gone haywire here. If we went to Slovakia for a few days, we could then return once the Pope has packed up and gone home."

"Slovenia," Hana said.

"Huh?"

"You said Slovakia."

The others agreed that she had.

"See, we don't even know where it is, or what country it

is… or who he is," Hana reasoned. "He might be a crazed axe murderer."

Mae cleared her throat. The others turned to her as she read from her phone. "Drago Lazar is the son of Alen Lazar. The Lazar company operates a chain of hotels and apartments wellness and spa centres, in… and excuse the pronunciation… Ljubljana, Bled, Portorož, Izola, Strunjan, and Piran in Slovenia. The company recently bought hotels in Croatia, Montenegro, France and Italy." Mae looked up at Hana. "Close your mouth. You'll catch flies."

"Are you sure it's him?"

Mae thrust out the phone at Hana and the others crowded round to look at it.

"Definitely him," Ada said.

"Hotter than the hottest day in hell," Frankie said. "And rich!"

"Well, why don't you run off to Slovenia with him?" Hana snapped.

"Because he's not interested in me. He's only asking us to go because he's interested in you."

That stopped Hana in her escalating mood tracks. "He is not."

The others looked at each other and laughed.

"He's totally into you," Mae said.

It was clear that Hana had never considered that.

"He looks at you like I look at ice cream," Frankie teased.

"And you know how she devours Brownie Batter," Ada said.

"Your problem is you think he's gorgeous, and he saved us so that adds extra points…" Mae said.

"But he's missing one major thing," Dina said.

Hana waited. "Yes?"

"He's not French." The girls said in unison.

Hana shrugged. That was that.

"I didn't see a French man getting us out of that burning hotel," Ada said.

"Oh for… he had a bloody key. It's not like he actually chewed through the door."

"My vote is still for the Slovenian."

Hana looked at her friends. "You guys actually want to go?"

A group nod.

Dina spoke first. "We can always come back to Paris. You can come back to Paris. But we've been offered this crazy opportunity for an adventure and, I think, in my admittedly limited experience, that we should grab it. I did in Tokyo. You made me grab it in Tokyo, and my life is all the better for it."

Mae shot her arm up into the air. "Hands up who votes for Slovenia."

Four arms raised. Only Hana kept hers firmly by her side.

"Are you seriously going to outvote me? On Paris?" Hana snapped. Her friends knew what Paris meant to her. "It might be better tomorrow."

Their arms stayed up in the air.

"You can't outvote me on Paris."

The arms remained up.

"How many hotels did you say his family owns?" Frankie laughed, and then jumped as she remembered something. "Hey, what time is it in Australia?"

"About eleven," Mae said.

Ada jumped up, grabbing her bag, and pulled out her iPad. Frankie started tapping on her phone. Even Mae pulled her phone out, if somewhat reluctantly.

Their ATAR results would be online.

Hana really didn't want to do this in front of the others. They'd spent years sharing everything, but all of a sudden she needed some privacy from them.

"I need to go to the loo but don't want to go alone. I'm a bit shaken up after everything. Will you come with me?"

Hana realised Dina was speaking to her. "Sure."

The two girls left the others to check their results and walked towards a bathroom at the back of the restaurant. Hana stepped aside at the door and gestured for Dina. "After you."

Dina stopped. "I don't actually need to. I just thought maybe you needed an excuse to do this solo."

Hana stared at Dina for a moment, moved by her intuition and kindness. "Thank you."

Dina smiled, and held the door open while Hana walked into the bathroom alone.

There were two cubicles, a mirrored vanity, and a Louis XV Bergere chair in the corner. It needed new upholstery but was otherwise beautiful. Only in McDonald's in Paris. She bet McDonald's in Slovenia didn't have that.

Hana sat and logged into her student site. It took a moment.

There it was. Her score.

Not as high as expected.

Not high enough.

In fact, it was a mark off what she needed.

Her heart sank.

Every dream she'd had went up in a puff of smoke. Paris. Study. Where her life would head after school. Nothing was as it should be. But she refused to cry. Not now. Everyone would know and she couldn't bear the sympathy.

She put her phone away, washed her face and combed her hair with her fingers.

She stared at herself in the mirror. Who was she? Really? She barely recognised herself. She was meant to be looking in the mirror, loving Paris, happy with her HSC marks, sure of where life was taking her.

She felt detached as she looked at herself. Same almond-shaped eyes, same freckles across her nose. But something had shifted. Despite everything being upside-down and wrong way up, she was okay. Strangely okay.

She headed out of the bathroom, relieved only Dina was there. She didn't feel as vulnerable with Dina.

Dina didn't say a word, but walked side by side with Hana, back to the others.

Mae was jumping up and down and hugging Ada, who was clearly happy.

"Ada must be on track to be a psychologist. How'd you go, Frankie?" Dina asked.

"Yeah, all good. Not sure it means anything, but I'm happy enough."

Dina turned to Mae. "Did you actually look?"

Mae gave her sister a cheeky grin. "Nope."

"You and Hana are so much alike," Dina said. "She refuses to look right now too."

"I'll look later." Hana glanced at Dina, grateful for the cover. And then turned to the others. "I was just in the loo… thinking… you're right. We need to go to Slovenia. I'm over Paris."

# CHAPTER Fourteen

Sometimes life can throw you an unexpected drama, such as a robbery or fire.

Other times, it can throw you something even more unexpected.

The girls grabbed a couple of hours sleep on the sofas in the foyer of the otherwise empty hotel. Despite the smell of smoke that still faintly lingered in the air, they had all fallen into an exhausted slumber until Drago woke them. They pulled themselves together and all piled into the van he'd arranged to take them to the airport.

"There will be breakfast and coffee on the plane," he promised.

Hana wondered if he'd had any sleep himself. Apart from the fatigue around his eyes, and the slight shadow of a beard, he certainly seemed to have energy. He chatted to their driver as they sped through the streets of early-morning Paris. Very few people were up. A few grungy teens hung outside an all-night club. Some early-morning workers were heading off to the daily grind. She spotted an impossibly chic woman wearing Chanel and carrying a small dog in her oversized tote. Hana shook her head. It was a sight she'd expected to see here in Paris, and yet the woman looked so out of place in the overcast early-morning light. And how ironic to see such a typically Parisian sight just as she was leaving Paris.

She slid down in her seat and rested her head against Dina. The other girls sat in the row behind then, quiet. Perhaps they'd fallen back asleep. None of them were exactly morning people. Apart from Dina, who'd spent her life at early-morning swim squad. She was the early riser of the group, but even she was silent this morning.

Hana listened to Drago's deep voice, speaking to the driver in what sounded like fluent French. Perhaps he could pass for French, she thought to herself. She certainly liked listening to him speak it. It was calming. Suddenly he turned his head and spoke to the girls.

"We're here."

Hana sat upright. That was quick. Too quick. Where had he taken them? She scanned the area and saw an airport sign.

"This isn't Charles de Gaulle Airport." Fear rushed through her body. What was going on? What if they were being kidnapped, sold into the slave trade or something?

Drago clearly had no inkling of the terror that was going through Hana's mind, because he calmly responded, "I couldn't get seats for all of us on a commercial flight at such short notice."

"Probably because of the Pope," Frankie mumbled from the back seat.

Drago continued. "So, I had to find a practical solution."

Hana liked practical solutions. She always tried to find practical solutions to problems. But he still hadn't explained what his practical solution actually was. Were they still going to Slovenia? Or were they going to be locked in a container and loaded onto a cargo plane and sent god-knows-where? Hana was really starting to panic that they'd got themselves into a situation that they shouldn't be in.

The van pulled up outside a building. A man in a suit approached the van and opened the door. Hana had no choice but to get out. The other girls followed, seemingly relaxed, apart from Ada, who always had a look of terror in her eyes when facing a new situation.

More men in suits appeared to take their luggage from the car and carry it inside.

Hana turned to Drago. "Where are we?"

He looked confused, as if she should know. "I'm sorry, I thought you realised. This is Paris Airport – Le Bourget."

"Yes, I got that from the sign, but why aren't we at Charles de Gaulle?"

"I couldn't get seats on a commercial flight."

"Then why are we at an airport?" There was no way they could do a runner with all their luggage. Not with the goons in suits nearby.

"So, I found a solution." Drago clearly thought he'd explained it.

"I didn't get the bloody memo explaining what that solution is," Hana snapped. "Explain what's going on."

The penny dropped. Drago looked apologetic. "I'm so sorry, I thought you understood. I couldn't get us all on a flight back to Ljubljana. So I hired a jet."

CHAPTER

# Fifteen

Mae was the first to speak. "Exqueeze me? A private jet?"

Drago laughed. "I know it sounds crazy—"

"Probably cause it is," Frankie said.

"It's convenient."

"That's what I always say about private jets: they're convenient," Mae quipped.

Drago clearly thought she was funny. "Then we are on the same page. And we will be back in Ljubljana in a couple of hours."

"Lubb-lee… where?" Dina asked.

"Ljubljana, Slovenia's capital."

"I really should have a rule about going to cities I can't pronounce," Hana said.

Mae did a funny dance and the others laughed. "I'm going on a private jet like a superstar!"

Hana stared at her friends in disbelief. They were all excited. Traitors!

She noticed another sign in a number of languages, including English.

Paris Airport – Le Bourget: the leading business airport in Europe.

They were seriously taking a private jet. And look at them all, in wrinkled clothes and unwashed hair, still smelling of smoke. Even Ada, who rarely had a hair out of place. Not that she was high maintenance, she was just born looking immaculate at all times. But this morning, her hair was knotted, and her eyes looked bleary.

Unlike Mae's eyes that were as wide as plates and filled with excitement. She raced up to Drago and grabbed his arm. "Tell me more about my private jet."

He laughed at her as she jumped up and down. "It's a corporate jet."

Mae threw both arms up in the air, in a victory pose. "Not yet seventeen: ticked private jet off the bucket list. Kicking it outta the park."

"Life goals," Frankie squealed.

Frankie and Dina were both caught up in Mae's enthusiasm and high-fived each other.

"Instagram worthy right there," Frankie said.

"Wait until I tell Ronin," Dina said.

The girls followed Drago and the porters into the building. Mae was skipping beside Drago, who seemed amused by her. Hana wished she'd stop. She was acting like a child. To be fair, Mae was younger. Moments like these made the two-year age gap seem pronounced.

Ada edged up beside Hana. "Are you okay with this?"

Hana realised that, despite her smiles, Ada was scared. She paused for a moment and thought about how to respond. What were they doing? Should she pull the plug on the whole mad adventure?

"I mean, are we doing the right thing?" Ada asked.

Hana looked at Drago joking around with Mae. She really liked him. She knew it was crazy. She knew they didn't actually know him, and yet she trusted him.

"I'm okay with this. I didn't really want to quit on Paris this early, but I like Drago and feel we can trust him."

Ada nodded. "Yes, I agree. I just wanted to check with you because you're the cautious one. It makes me feel better for you to trust him too."

"If you don't want to do this, I'll stop it immediately."

Ada's chin lifted slightly, a determined tilt. "I'm fine."

Hana gave Ada a quick hug. "It's nuts, but let's just enjoy it. I think he's really trying to do the right thing by us."

"And I'll probably never have another opportunity to board a private jet."

Hana rolled her eyes at her friend. "Ada, with your looks, you could have private jets lined up waiting."

Ada screwed her pretty face up. "Once is fun… I'm happy with that."

Hana just stared at her friend. She was such a stunning package but wanted a quiet life where she slid by unnoticed. Hana herself was an introvert, but Ada took that to new heights.

They were ushered into a stylish airport lounge, decorated in deep chocolate fabric and dark wood. The girls made themselves comfortable, and a waiter soon arrived with juice and pastries. They could see the tarmac now, outside the large lounge windows, with a number of sleek planes parked nearby.

Hana watched Drago shake hands with the airport staff. They obviously knew him, and he paused to chat to a number of them.

She was astounded by his maturity. He couldn't be that much older than her, and yet he was so self-assured. Not arrogant, but levelheaded.

She liked that. Hana had always been levelheaded too. While many of her peers were experimenting with drugs and drink and sex, she was renovating a house she'd inherited from her grandparents. She wasn't interested in a lot of things her peers were interested in. Apart from Mae, Frankie, Ada and now Dina, it was difficult finding common ground with most people her own age, especially boys.

Dina was the first to speak as she gestured for the other girls to huddle in. "I think we need to touch base and just make sure everyone is okay with this. It's an outrageous thing to do."

Hana nodded. "I agree. Are you okay with it?"

"I think it's exciting, but I also know that you and Ada might have some reservations."

"I'm okay," Ada said. "I always have reservations, about everything, but honestly, I'm kind of relieved to leave Paris."

Hana didn't want to admit that she was too, so just said. "It's not every day you get to fly on a private jet."

Mae was jiggling up and down. It was driving Hana nuts. It actually looked like she needed to go to the bathroom.

"I am so excited," Mae said.

"Really?" said Hana. "I never could've picked it."

Frankie jumped up. "Come and burn off some steam, Mae, and take some photos of me."

Mae grabbed Frankie's phone off her and followed her to a section of the window with a good view of the planes outside. Hana turned her attention to Drago, who was making his way back to them, with their passports in hand.

"Is everyone ready to board?"

"That was quick," Dina said. "C'mon, Ada, before you change your mind."

Two serious looking women in grey suits greeted them and whisked them all out of the lounge and onto the tarmac. Even Mae calmed down for a moment… until she actually saw their plane.

"Holy moly, wait until I tell Alex!" With that she zipped her mouth. Mae ignored Hana's inquisitive stare and ran up ahead.

Hana wasn't sure the others had heard but reminded herself to ask Mae who Alex was later. For now, she was too busy having her mind blown as she walked up the steps to board their flight. It really was surreal.

The plane was a small, sleek Hawker that seated eight passengers. The layout was simple with two sets of two seats facing each other on either side of the plane, a longer lounge seat at the back on one side and another single seat opposite it. The seats were white leather and the detailing glossy mahogany wood. There was a bathroom at the back of the plane and a small galley with catering already laid out on a mahogany counter for the girls to help themselves to once they were airborne.

The thrill of boarding a private jet cured their exhaustion. The girls squealed and claimed seats, and then swapped seats again and again. The plane was warm, so coats and scarves came off and were stored with bags. Only Hana contained herself. She slipped into one of the seats and buckled her belt.

Once they'd boarded, Drago sat next to Ada for a few minutes, chatting about what to expect and the plane's safety standards, which were apparently "exceptionally high". Hana watched as Ada broke out into a relaxed smile. Drago gave her arm a pat and then turned to the others to include them.

"I have created a program for you."

Ada smiled even more.

He extracted some papers from a leather pouch and handed one to each of the five girls. Hana ran her fingers across hers in silent approval. It was thick, cream with bronze lettering on it. How on earth did he get these printed so quickly?

"As you know, Hana would prefer to be in Paris," Drago said. "But the Pope has… how do you say in Australia? Buggered that up?"

Everyone, even Hana, laughed.

Drago gave them a cheeky grin. "I Googled that. Anyway," he continued, "I spoke to my family and explained the circumstances, of the Pope and the hotel fire. We want you to be our guests in our hotel for two nights in Ljubljana. It is a wonderful city, the capital of Slovenia. I'm certain you'll like it. From there, if you would like to visit Lake Bled, I would be honoured to take you. I can also help you return to Paris once the Pope has… er…"

"Buggered off," Mae finished.

He laughed. "Exactly. Anyway, on that paper are all the contact details of the hotel. This plane has Internet so if you want to contact your families… or boyfriends… please do so."

His eyes rested on Hana and she felt an unfamiliar stirring in her gut.

"None of us have boyfriends," Mae blurted. "Oh, apart from my sister. Dina's boyfriend is Hana's brother."

Drago took a moment to wrap his head around that, and then glancing at Hana, he stood. "Please just relax and enjoy your flight."

Drago took one of the single seats at the front and started to make a phone call. The plane began to move, off the apron and along the taxiway. The girls all fell silent, the enormity of what they were doing kicking in.

"No turning back now," Ada said.

The plane moved into position on the runway and paused, and they waited, before finally the engine fired up, a roar beneath them. And then, a full burst of power as it began hurtling along the runway, faster, faster, until the nose tilted up, the ground dropped away, and they were airborne.

"Holy crapoly!" Mae squealed.

Hana stared out the window as Paris grew smaller and smaller and then disappeared as the plane was enveloped by clouds. Her heart raced. Despite herself, Hana was excited. It was incredible. It did feel adventurous doing this. She was upset Paris hadn't worked out the way she dreamt it would, and yet, this was truly exciting.

Before long, they heard the sound of the wheels being tucked away and the plane levelled out. Moments later, the seatbelt sign went off.

Mae immediately jumped up. "I'm starved, superstars. Who wants breakfast?"

Frankie and Dina joined Mae at the buffet. They piled their plates high with food. Ada started munching down on a croissant. That was a good sign.

"Here, you need to eat too." Dina appeared in front of Hana with a pain au chocolat and a freshly squeezed orange juice.

"I won't say no to that. Thanks."

"Girl's gotta eat. Even when she's on a private jet with a gorgeous guy" Dina gave Hana a wink and Hana couldn't help but laugh. It was all too surreal.

About twenty minutes into the flight, that gorgeous guy came and sat opposite Hana.

"How are you flying?" he asked.

"Well, if you've been on one private jet, you've been on them all."

Drago laughed. "It's not my regular mode of transport. It's just it was impossible to get flights for you all on such short notice."

"So, you don't own this jet?"

"No. My family uses the company that owns this jet sometimes.

For convenience." "That's what I say about Uber. Maybe I'll own my own jet… when I grow up."

He smiled at her, perfect teeth, full lips. Hana was awash with the strongest urge to kiss him. Instead, she turned her head to look out the window, mortified.

"Look at that cloud," she said.

"How about you, Hana? Tell me about yourself."

"What do you already know?" Hana was back on familiar and more comfortable turf. She never shied away from the truth. "You took our passports earlier to sort this flight out, so you have my full name. Did you Google me?"

"Yes," he admitted.

"And?"

"You're the daughter of Hiro Honda, who owns Hi Ho." His eyes lit up. "A very cool brand."

"You know it?"

"It's not in Slovenia, but I bought some Hi Ho shorts when I was in Hawaii last year. I liked them so much I bought more online." He stared at her for a moment. "Did you Google me?"

"Of course. Mae did. There's no way we'd get on a private jet with just anyone." Hana gave him a cheeky grin.

"So this is a first?"

"No… a third or fourth, but the others didn't work out well."

They laughed. The energy between them was thick with attraction, but while Hana was smart and savvy, she was also inexperienced with guys. She was in very unfamiliar territory, not just on the plane, but also with him. Prior to meeting Drago, flirting had been a fun thing she'd done regularly, with no intention of following through. With Drago, she didn't know where it would lead, and that was unnerving.

Drago pushed his hair back off his face, searching for the

right words. “So, we have discovered that we both come from successful families, but that’s our families, not us. I’d like to know more about you. Not your father or his company. You.”

This took Hana by surprise. “Why?”

“Because the moment I laid eyes on you, I thought you were lovely. Any conversations we’ve had, I see that you’re smart and… what’s the English word? Feisty?”

Hana simultaneously blushed and cursed the heat across her cheeks. “Good answer,” she managed. “Your English is perfect. Did you go to an international school?”

“Boarding school in the UK,” Drago said. “I’m lucky that I’ve travelled a lot. I’ve always had great travel experiences and people have been kind.”

“Is that why you’ve offered us this trip? To be kind?”

Drago shrugged. “It’s important to keep an eye out for each other in life. I promise you, my offer for a great hotel experience stands. No expectations. How do you say in English, no strings attached?”

Hana nodded. “No strings. Exactly. And that’s good. That works for me. Thanks.”

It was a relief to know that this trip came without any strings. He was being kind and didn’t expect anything in return.

And that worked for Hana.

She had to turn and look out the window again, to escape his gaze. No strings suited her, but why she felt so disappointed was confusing.

CHAPTER

# Sixteen

Hana envied Frankie with her battered backpack. She was certain the cobbled pavement was going to crack the wheels of her Louis Vuitton case. It had been a gift from her dad. Of course, she'd fallen fabulously in love the moment she laid eyes on it, but she'd discovered that during the trip she'd been so concerned about it going missing enroute or being pummelled by baggage handlers that she was starting to think Frankie had the right idea. Or Dina, with her simple grey suitcase. She'd never get away with the pink one painted with a peace sign that Mae was dragging behind her—Mae's style was all her own. At least she wasn't dragging as much luggage around as Ada, but then Ada's baggage was excessive and not just her two large suitcases.

Drago had one small, stylish carry-on that she had given the once-over and immediately approved of. She also approved the way his jeans hugged his butt and strong thighs, his Maison Kitsuné jacket and Lacoste sneakers. He might not be French, but he wore French well. He clearly had money, but then she came from money too. That wasn't important to Hana. And she was well aware that only the rich could say that. But she'd been raised to not feel guilty about her family's money, and to always be humble and give back where possible. Sure, she liked her designer labels, but generally if she bought something expensive, she kept it for years.

Private jet aside, Drago wasn't flashy. What she was drawn

to was the fact that he was a gentleman. She knew it was old-fashioned of her to look for that in a guy, but chivalry really was dying in her generation. Hana wanted to fall in love with a gentleman, someone with manners. Obviously, she didn't want a guy who opened doors for her but also expected her to cook. The guy she was waiting for would appreciate an equal, and yet still be respectful of those innate differences between the sexes.

She liked that he was kind to them all, and had them laughing, and explained interesting things. She liked him for all those reasons, not just because he was tall with incredible full lips. Although that certainly helped.

Actually, that was the problem. If he'd just been nice and unattractive, perhaps she would still be in Paris searching for her French experience, which may or may not include a French guy.

She reminded herself, that wasn't actually true. She'd been outvoted by her friends. She'd had no choice but to leave Paris. They'd all betrayed her and now she was dragging her bags across the cobblestones in Ljubljana instead.

She looked up, soaking in the view around her for the first time. The narrow street was lined with large stone pots, containing shrubs and trees, mostly bare for winter. Vines crawled up the walls of immaculately restored buildings, in a mix of gorgeous architectural styles.

It was beautiful.

Drago waited for the girls to catch up and indicated to the building in front of them. "Our hotel."

Hana stared up at the old building in front of them. It wasn't at all what she expected, and the starkness of the brick exterior seemed at odds with the villas in warm colours nearby.

"It was once a warehouse," he said. "The building is from the seventeenth century."

He led them through the double glass doors and into the foyer, then turned and watched Hana for her reaction. The hotel was nothing like she expected. Her imagination had flipped between an awful hotel like the one in Paris, and some cheesy chain hotel, that had dated décor and buffet breakfasts. It was neither of these. It was like nothing she'd seen before.

"Uber cool," Frankie said.

"Bloody hell," said Dina.

The old warehouse was now a sleek and modern boutique hotel, but with an art deco touch. It had exposed brick walls, and parquet floors with a sparse layout. The wood, brick and stone features were softened by the natural hues used in the furnishings and fittings. The place was flooded with natural light and Hana looked up to see a glass rooftop that included an infinity pool.

"There's a swimming pool above us."

Drago nodded. "The people in the pool can also look down here. If they wear... how do you say? ... googles?"

The girls laughed.

"Close," Frankie said. "Goggles."

Drago joined their laughter. "It's my fourth language so you must excuse it."

The girls stopped laughing and instead all looked embarrassed. Hana made a mental note to brush up on her French and Japanese.

It was clear that the staff knew they were coming. A receptionist gave them a wave. A woman approached with a couple of keycards and a smile. She was about thirty and as cool as the hotel itself, in a black wool crepe dress with large silver earrings and grey suede Chloé ankle boots. Her dark hair was pulled back into a ponytail and she completed her look with a deep red lipstick.

"Welcome to Ljubljana," she said. "I'm Irena, the day manager."

Drago introduced the group. "Irena, this is Hana, Mae, Dina, Ada and Frankie. They are our special VIP guests."

"If you need anything at all, please let me know." Irena passed the keycards to the girls and then gestured for one of the porters to come over. "Marko will show you to your rooms."

Drago turned to the girls. "Please settle in. The hotel is in the historic centre of Ljubljana, if you feel like exploring this afternoon. There's a lot to see nearby. Ask at reception for tourist maps." His eyes rested on Hana. "I'm meeting some friends tonight, if you'd all like to come out with us?"

Frankie answered for her. "We'd love to meet some locals. That would be great."

"Excellent. I'll see you here at seven." And with that he turned and exited the hotel, leaving the girls to follow Marko into the glass lift and to their rooms on the third floor.

There were two rooms for the girls to choose from. One had a queen and a single, so Frankie, Mae and Ada grabbed that together. Hana was relieved. She was still feeling annoyed with the group for outvoting her on Paris, even though in the end she'd agreed to leave too. Plus, her issues with Frankie were snowballing. Dina was the one friend she could handle at the moment, so they took the room with two singles.

The room was lovely and large with white brick walls, pale wood floors and matching single bed frames. The bathroom was white marble and minimalist, with a floor to ceiling glass shower, underfloor heating and heated towel rails. While the suite was, to use Frankie's words, uber cool, it was also a cosy retreat from the cold Ljubljana winter.

The clean lines and soft hues appealed to Hana, who felt immediately at home. Which was followed by a tug of annoyance. She was meant to feel at home in Paris, not a city she could barely pronounce.

Alone with Dina in this stunning room, Hana suddenly felt she could relax. Dina sensed this, watching her from the bathroom door.

"Do you need some time alone?"

"No, I'm happy to be sharing with you."

"Did Frankie do something to you?"

Hana shook her head. "It's just her obsession with social media is annoying me. I get that it pays for this trip, but there have been a few times when she's so focused about it being a great Instagram moment that she's not noticing it might not be a good moment for one of us."

"She really wasn't taking an Instagram shot of Ada being mugged."

"I know that. I admit I jumped to that conclusion, but with good reason. Remember how I was so upset when we arrived at the Paris hotel? Well, she took a photo and posted it without my permission, and it got 24000 likes." Hana grabbed her phone and opened the app, scrolling through photos until she found the one of her mournfully looking at the hotel. Frankie had captioned it Broken Dreams with a series of hashtags that included #awfulhotels #traveldreams #brokendreams #devastatedtravelbuddy and, the worst one, #heartbrokenhana.

"Oh wow, that's not cool. Have you spoken to her about this?" Dina asked.

"Not yet. I haven't had time. It's just been one shitstorm after another since we arrived in Paris."

Dina was scrolling back through the rest of Frankie's account.

"I'm checking she hasn't posted any awful ones of me."

"She hasn't. There are some group ones we all agreed to, but that's the first photo of any of us she's posted without permission."

Dina understood how private Hana was. She didn't even have her own public account.

"Oh my god, she posted photos of the fire."

Hana gave Dina an 'I know' look. "I almost had to drag her out of the burning building."

"No wonder you're upset with her. But you guys are so close. Try and resolve it. Don't let it impact your trip."

Hana walked over to the window and stared out at the charming Baroque buildings and the cobbled street below.

"You're upset about Paris too?"

Hana nodded. "This view is better. This room, this hotel… how can it be better than Paris?"

"It's not better. It's just different. In Paris you were seeing everything through the lens of preconceived expectations. Kind of like me and an empty Japanese tatami room."

Hana laughed. "Ye olde tatami room lesson."

"It was a huge lesson for me but maybe one you need to learn too. Without the tatami."

"You're right. I feel like I need to regroup. Maybe I'll take off by myself for a few hours."

"Good idea. Time alone is important. I had that in Japan when I went to the pool each day. It really helped me sort out how I was feeling about Japan."

"And about my brother," Hana grinned.

"Yep, him too."

Dina joined Hana at the window, and they stood side by side staring out at the view.

“It really is beautiful,” Dina said.

“It really is,” Hana said. “How annoying.”

CHAPTER

# Seventeen

Hana stared down at her feet. She was standing on yet another manhole cover with a bronzed image of a castle and a dragon on it. The castle she got. It was impossible to miss the medieval castle perched on top of the hill, just above the historic area of the city. Clearly the castle was important. But dragons? Why were there so many mythical beasts plastered around the city. Hana pulled out the tourist pamphlet that she'd taken from the hotel.

> *Slovenia is a wonderful country to visit, with warm people, amazing scenery, and excellent transport. And it's still reasonably cheap, certainly in comparison to its neighbours, Italy and Austria. The capital of Slovenia is Ljubljana, which has garnered a reputation as "the new Prague." But Ljubljana isn't "the new" anything. It doesn't try to be. It's a jewel of a city, rich in history and culture. It's small enough to walk around the old area and, as a university city, it's young and vibrant. The locals are laid-back and friendly.*

That was all very nice and informative, but what about the dragons? Hana spotted a section.

> *Ljubljana is a Dragon Spotter's paradise. Dragons are everywhere. According to legend, Jason and the Argonauts sailed into Ljubljana and found a monster in a lake. Jason slew the "Dragon of Ljubljana", but its image remains emblazoned on everything from drainpipes to T-shirts. The most famous*

*monument is the Dragon Bridge, guarded by four bronze dragons. Local legend says the dragons wave their tails when a virgin crosses the bridge.*

Hana looked up and noticed a bridge in the distance. Hilarious. All four would be waving their tails if she crossed. She hadn't even come close to having sex. She decided to bring the girls back to the bridge later, for a laugh.

The dragon mystery solved, she shoved the pamphlet back into her bag and made her way along the river, past market stalls selling vegetables and foodstuff and artisan goods. Her pace slowed as the smell of fresh pastries, breads and cheeses drew her in. She had nowhere to go, no place to be. She enjoyed exploring the laneways of stalls. Time disappeared as she paused to look at bottles of pumpkin oil and to sample a spoon of honey.

"From local hives," the stallholder explained. "Where are you from?" She was a large woman, with grey tendrils of hair escaping a pulled back bun. She was wearing layers of warm clothes, a scarf and fingerless gloves.

"I'm from Australia."

The woman beamed, warm creases around her eyes and mouth. "I like Australians."

Hana smiled. She couldn't help herself. "I like Slovenians."

It was true. She did like them. Everyone she'd met so far had been friendly. A number of stallholders chatted to her in good English, making Hana feel embarrassed by her lack of Slovenian. To be fair, she didn't realise the country existed until yesterday, but still, she really needed to learn a few words.

She picked up a small wooden board with what appeared to be a folktale painted on it. The woman had quite a display of the boards with a number of different images painted on the front.

"This is panjske končnice. It is panel from the front of bee hives," she explained.

"Oh, I see. And what are the paintings on the front of them?"

"It's a story, usually a folk legend. It helps the beekeeper remember every hive."

Hana laughed. "Clever." She picked up another panel that showed a man carrying an old woman in a basket on his back. Then he placed her into what appeared to be a barrel and from the other side, he pulls out a much younger woman.

"That one says…the old man who gives his wife away and gets a younger one." The stall owner gave a grunt. "You are too young to understand."

"No, I understand," Hana said quietly. "How do I say, 'how much for this' in Slovenian?" No time like the present to learn those few words.

The woman spoke slowly. "Koliko je to."

Hana tried it. "Koliko je to?"

The woman said it again. "Koliko je to."

Hana repeated. "Koliko je to?"

The woman clapped her hands together. "Perfect."

She told Hana the price and Hana gave her some euro and tucked the panel into her bag. It was a gift for Ronin. It would amuse him. Or really anger him. Either way, it was appropriate.

She checked the time. It was after lunch. No wonder she was hungry. She asked the woman where she could eat.

"Do you want good Slovenian goulash?"

Hana had never tried goulash. She didn't even really know what it was, but, in that moment, high on honey and bee panels and learning her first Slovenian word, it sounded perfect.

The woman gave her directions to a small restaurant nearby that she promised would be the best goulash Hana had ever tasted.

Not hard, seeing she'd never tasted it, but Hana thanked her profusely and headed off down the street, across the first bridge (there were a few) and then down the first small laneway on the right.

The directions were perfect. The cafe was clearly signed and open for business.

Hana entered and had the warmth of the nearby fireplace hit her. The restaurant was small, with about five tables, two of which were occupied. A woman wearing an apron over a sweater with rolled up sleeves waved her in.

"Zdravo." She quickly realised Hana was an English speaker. "Welcome, welcome."

The woman ushered Hana to an empty table for two in the corner, took her coat and hung it over the other chair. She handed Hana a menu and then poured her a glass of water. Hana glanced at the menu but was unable to read it so handed it back, and simply said, "Goulash?"

For all Hana knew there were ten types of goulash on the menu, but the woman gave a friendly nod and disappeared into the kitchen.

Hana sat in stillness for a moment. She took in the heavy beams overhead, the large wooden clock on the wall, the dated furniture and mustard-coloured tablecloths.

The sound of a loud rumbling laugh in the kitchen. Male. Followed by the woman's laugh, from her belly.

A couple around her own age were in the other corner, deep in conversation.

A man sat alone nearby, reading a book.

And the smell. The deep, rich smell of food and spices and dishes she didn't recognise but that made her mouth water.

The strangest feeling washed over Hana. She didn't

understand what it was, but she liked it. She felt… not happy. It was less complex. Content? How was it that she felt so comfortable in this unfamiliar place? She liked what she'd seen so far of Ljubljana. She enjoyed having time alone to clear her head. She was happier in this moment, at a rustic old table with a mustard tablecloth (a colour really low on her list of likeable colours) than she'd been, even for a second, in Paris.

Why? How could that be?

She had no answers, but then, for once, didn't really feel she needed an answer right now. She was happy to enjoy the moment. She knew it was silly, but it felt like an initiation into another facet of adulthood. Alone, in the strange country, the funny little restaurant, and the table. Alone. And good with that.

The woman reappeared and a dish was placed in front of her, a large plate of what she would now identify as goulash.

"You like this?" The woman asked.

Hana looked up at her and smiled. "First time."

The woman grinned. "You start with the best. We call this segediner. That is beef and sauerkraut and many spices."

Hana loaded up her fork and took a mouthful. It was hot, heavy and rich. She could taste paprika, garlic and caraway seeds. She looked at the woman again and nodded. "Delicious."

The woman seemed pleased with that and left Hana to her meal. Hana realised how hungry she was and ploughed into it. The goulash warmed her to her core. It comforted her, and even in this strange environment, she felt at ease. It wasn't a dish she'd want often, but it was perfect today, in this moment.

She thought about everything while she ate. She'd had a rough few days. Paris had sucked. Nothing about it was what she expected. Admittedly, getting her HSC results there had really cast a shadow over everything. She'd always pictured having the best time in Paris and briefly pausing to check her results, feeling pleased that she'd blitzed it, which would get her into her chosen degree. Not for a second could she have imagined all the drama in Paris. She could have bounced back from one or two things, but a whole chain of upsetting events, topped by her disappointing ATAR.

She was left feeling confused by the city she'd always dreamt about.

Nothing was as it should be.

Not even Drago. If she was honest, she'd always expected to have a holiday romance in Paris. It was a part of the vision she'd built up around the trip. So how was it that she did meet a handsome, nice guy only to find out that he comes from a country she'd never so much as registered existed before yesterday?

Hana really didn't want to diminish all he'd done for them—the trip, the free hotel, the opportunity to experience all of this. It's just he wasn't what she expected. Also, a little voice inside her kept asking why he was even doing this for them all? Surely no one was that kind? He'd said no strings, but was that the truth? Did he expect something in return?

She looked down at her empty plate and ran the last piece of crusty bread along the edge, mopping up the sauce and licking it. Delicious. The whole day was delicious. Drago was delicious, damn it. Hana was a bundle of conflicted emotions. Her grandmother popped into her mind. Oh, how she missed her Baba.

Her grandmother had come to Australia during their family crisis. She'd arrived unannounced; although Hana had a sneaking suspicion her father had actually arranged it. He knew his mother would bring a sense of calm and order into their fractured and chaotic world.

After Ronin's arrest, things changed again. Obviously, no charges were pressed. Their father made it clear that his priority was the family, not the business. His son, not the design. He moved back into the home, although into a guest bedroom. All four family members were back under the one roof.

But nothing had really been resolved. At least not for Hana, who had a million unanswered questions and no one addressing them.

One day, she was helping her grandmother with dinner, and explained how she was feeling. Her grandmother shared a story with her.

"A philosopher saw an old man jump into a raging river and be swept over a waterfall. The philosopher was sure the old man would be drowned so went in search of his body. Miraculously, the old man was found alive and unharmed. The philosopher thought it was a miracle. When he asked the old man how he'd survived he said, 'I adapted myself to the water, I didn't fight it. Without thinking, I allowed myself to be shaped by it. Plunging into the swirl, I moved with the swirl, I came out with the swirl. This is how I survived the river'."

Hana stared at her, confused. "Wakaranai. I don't understand."

Her grandmother smiled. "Stop fighting the river. Go with the flow."

"You sound like a hippy." Hana thought for a moment. "Is that an old Japanese folktale?"

"No, no. Chinese," Her grandmother chuckled. "Confucius, I think. But I like that story."

Hana realised she needed to take her grandmother's advice again right now. She couldn't solve everything immediately. Nothing was going to plan, but she could let go and go with the flow. After all, she was happier right now than she'd been in days. Or maybe longer. That much was clear. It was because of the people she'd met, the experiences she'd had, and the goulash.

In Ljubljana… not in Paris.

Warm from the food and the open fireplace, she felt a new sense of purpose. Her life was just beginning, and just because it wasn't going to plan, didn't mean wonderful things weren't happening. She would change her university course preferences or find a different pathway into her degree. She'd work it out. She would still be a designer.

And she'd sort out her friendship with Frankie. They'd never fought before this trip. Frankie was easy going and had a huge heart. Hana hated that she was judging her friend so harshly.

She'd also enjoy Slovenia. Being here was an unexpected gift. How many people had the opportunity to fly on a private plane and stay at a beautiful hotel, in a wonderful city, all provided by a very nice guy with incredible hair? She needed to step up and enjoy it.

She paid the woman, giving her the universal sign language for delicious, rubbing her belly and a thumbs up. The woman responded with a hearty chuckle, and helped Hana slip back into her coat. Hana buttoned her jacket, wrapped her scarf around her neck, and stepped back out into the cold winter air, ready to go where the river took her.

CHAPTER

# Eighteen

"Frankie, can I talk to you?"

The girls were in the hotel entrance, waiting for Drago to arrive. They were all in high spirits from an enjoyable day in Slovenia's capital and now looking forward to a night out. And they'd dressed for it. The other girls had been shopping while Hana had been eating goulash, so were decked out in new gear.

Ada was in head to toe black: black jeans, black tight turtleneck and her black boots. Over it all was a burgundy trench coat.

Frankie had on a cable knit sweater, boots and a wool mini skirt that accentuated her long legs. She also wore a cute hat and new grey jacket that was apparently a "total bargain".

Dina looked casual and cool in her usual jeans, boots and jacket, but with a new navy wool fedora.

And then there was Mae, her pink hair sticking out the bottom of a white beanie with a pom pom on top. She wore patterned tights, under a fraying denim skirt, with a hooded puffer jacket over the top.

Hana herself had changed into a wool mini dress, with tights and boots and a poncho jacket over the top. She looked around now. Everyone looked great and seemed to be in a much better mood than they had been for days.

She decided to call it the Ljubljana effect.

Hana pulled Frankie aside.

"Hey, I want to apologise for the other day. I know you didn't take that photo for Instagram."

Frankie's face lit up and she threw her arms around Hana, pulling her in for a hug. "Thanks Hana. I appreciate your apology."

Hana hugged her back. "I mean, you understand why I jumped to that conclusion though, don't you?" She wanted to broach the other photo Frankie had posted without permission gently.

Frankie pulled back, the smile wiped and her eyes wary. "What do you mean?"

"Well, you're always taking photos and posting them." Hana was easing into the part where she confronted her about that photo.

"My Insta account pays for this trip," Frankie said defensively.

This wasn't going quite as well as she'd hoped. "I know, and I absolutely get that. But you can see how I jumped to that conclusion?"

Frankie pursed her lips. "Not really, but you've always had a tendency to be black and white about things."

That threw Hana. How was this becoming about her?

"So, you don't think you cross any lines with what you post?"

Frankie's eyes narrowed. "I post once or twice a day. Always have. Nothing has changed except how successful I am. Maybe that's your problem."

"You really think that? You really don't know why I'm upset?" But before Hana had a chance to bring up the photo of her that Frankie had posted without permission, the hotel lobby filled with voices and Drago arrived. And he had with him two of the most gorgeous-looking guys Hana had ever seen.

Even Frankie was suddenly smiling again. The girls met Bor and Gal.

Gal was Bor's younger brother, and still at high school. Bor went to the University of Ljubljana, where he was on the same ice hockey team as Drago.

"We thought we'd just see where the night takes us," Drago said. "How do you say, go with the flow?"

Hana, who thought about her grandmother's story, saw that as a sign to just forget her issues with Frankie for now and enjoy the night. The others were obviously in agreement about going with the flow too. They all fell into step and headed out into the street. Drago waited until last to walk beside Hana.

"You look beautiful."

Hana was grateful for the dark night, so she could blush in private. "Thank you."

"Did you have a nice day?"

"I did. I spent some time alone. I went to the Central Market, and then I tasted goulash for the first time."

Drago laughed. "Wow, that's really experiencing Slovenia on your first day. Goulash. What did you think?"

"I liked it."

"Then you pass the test."

"I'm being tested?"

"No, I don't believe in tests."

Hana pushed her ATAR to the back of her mind. "So, you're at university?"

"Yes. I'm in my second year of a business degree."

"You don't actually work for the hotel?" Hana was trying to make sense of someone his age being at the Paris hotel.

"I do some work for the company. My father believes we should all contribute, but he's also preparing me to work there after university."

"So, you were working in Paris?"

"My father bought L'Hotel Bouchard. I was there over the

weekend finalising things with Madame Bouchard before she leaves. She is moving to Strasbourg, near her daughter. I often oversee things for my father."

"You're expected to go into the family business then, when you graduate?"

"I don't think my parents expect me to, but they would like me to. And I want to. I love hotels. Will you go into your family business?"

Hana shook her head. "No. My brother already has. He runs the Tokyo office."

"What are your plans?"

It was a huge question for Hana right now, not that Drago realised that. "I want to study design," she said. "I love interiors. I want to be an interior designer."

The penny dropped for Drago. "That's why you were so upset by L'Hotel Bouchard?"

"Yes. I really wanted to stay somewhere special in Paris. I knew it couldn't be expensive. My friends can't afford it. But I figured I could still find somewhere unique, with elegant touches."

"Instead you found L'Hotel Bouchard." Drago laughed. "I feel so bad. If I'd known you were coming, I would have renovated."

"Well, I did end up in the one renovated room."

"The details of the sale took a few months and my father was adamant that he couldn't stay in the other rooms when he visited. You wait until you see what they plan to do with it. It will be a superb hotel once it has been restored."

"I can imagine. It definitely has the potential."

"It won't smell damp either." Drago nudged Hana with his shoulder.

Hana giggled. "That's a good start."

"What do you think of the hotel here?"

Hana's face lit up. "It's wonderful, such a unique hotel. Clean lines, stylish furnishings and fittings, and some very cool design choices."

"That's a great review!"

"I read it on TripAdvice," Hana teased.

The group turned a corner and before them lay one of the prettiest sights Hana had ever seen. The girls all squealed their delight, which made Drago and his friends laugh.

"I'm glad you approve," Drago said. "There are a few Christmas markets in Ljubljana, but this one in Prešeren Square is the most famous."

The large square was lit up with lights strung from every tree, every building. In the centre was an enormous exquisitely decorated tree. Hana looked up and realised that the lights above them were shaped like planets and stars, the whole universe strung out and lighting up the city sky. It was crowded, with people shopping at the many stalls that sold sweets and cookies and artisan goods. Food stalls and bars lined the outer edge of the market, with groups of people milling around, drinking and laughing.

They moved with the crowd, past wooden stalls selling ornaments and an array of goods from sugar cookies to winter hats. The smell of pastries, roasted chestnuts and hot mulled wine hung in the air. Drago and Bor bought mulled wine for everyone, although both Mae and Gal passed theirs to the others.

"It's called kuhano vino in Slovenian," Drago explained.

Drago's eyes were locked on Hana as she took a sip, and Hana couldn't be sure if it was the hot wine and cinnamon that sent a torrent of heat through her body, or his dark, long-lashed eyes.

"What do you think?" he asked her.

It took her a moment to realise he was talking about the mulled wine. "How do you say spicy in Slovenian?" she said with a sly smile.

He raised an eyebrow. "Začinjeno."

"Začinjeno," she repeated, looking into his eyes.

The rest of their group had moved ahead, through the crowds. Hana saw the Dragon Bridge that she'd read about up ahead, thrilled she'd get to show her friends.

But before Hana could say anything, Bor's voice rang out, "Come on, girls. Now we must find out if you are virgins."

CHAPTER

# Nineteen

Mae, Dina, Ada and Frankie all faced Bor, a wall of unified disbelief.

Mae was the first to speak. "Where we come from, that type of talk will get you arrested."

"Or slapped," Frankie added.

"Was something lost in translation?" asked Dina.

Drago was clearly embarrassed and tried to retrieve the situation. He gave Bor a slap across the back of his head and chastised him in Slovenian first, and then said, "Man, I've told you to have more English lessons. You are so embarrassing." He turned to the girls and tried to explain. "I think we're having a cultural difference here, and Bor's bad English doesn't help. See the bridge up ahead?"

Hana decided to help him out a bit. "With the dragons at each end? I've already read about it." She pulled the pamphlet from her bag and opened to the section that described the Dragon Bridge.

Drago nodded. "It's called the Dragon Bridge. Very original. You may have noticed that there are a lot of dragons here in Ljubljana?"

"Hard to miss," Dina said.

"It is believed that the founder of this city slayed a dragon. Anyway, we have a weird thing for dragons. In fact, there aren't just four dragons on the bridge. If you want to come and have a look, there are sixteen more. But according to local legend, and this is what Bor was talking about, when a virgin crosses the bridge, the dragons will wag their tails."

Hana passed the pamphlet to Mae. "It's true. I read it earlier today."

"Bor was not making a suggestion, but rather making a joke." Drago shot his friend a look. "But he's not very funny."

Bor looked suitably chastened. "I'm not funny. I'm famous for not being funny." He smiled at the girls, genuinely sorry. "Sorry. I didn't mean to make you uncomfortable."

Frankie was the first one to step forward. "Don't worry about it. Apology accepted. I know a genuine apology when I hear one."

Hana felt the dig at her.

Mae was scanning the pamphlet. "Okay, Bor, you're forgiven, but I still can't help but think this legend of yours is a little misogynistic. Do the dragons wave their tails for males as well as females?"

Bor looked somewhat embarrassed. "Only female. In fact, I've never considered how inappropriate this is until today. I should start a petition."

Mae turned to her friends. "How do we address misogyny while still respecting cultural differences?" She threw her hands up in the air. "There are so many confusing layers to being a feminist."

Dina looped her arm around Mae's neck and pulled her in for a hug. "You're sixteen. You're doing okay."

"Let's go see the bridge." Frankie walked ahead of them.

Drago looked at Hana, gauging her mood. "Is that okay?"

"Of course. I'd love to see the dragons close up." She gave him a sexy side-glance. "Just don't expect me to cross the bridge, because what those dragons might know about me is none of your business."

Now it was Drago's turn to blush, Hana noticed, thanks to a street lamp above him.

They caught up to the others as the group all made their way to the bridge. Even at night the bridge still drew large crowds of tourists.

They watched as groups of girls crossed, giggling to each other and more often than not, playing to the boys they were with.

"What hope is there when our generation is happy to play into the belief that a woman's virginity is some sort of currency?" Mae sniffed.

Gal stared at her as one would a work of art. "You are so cool."

Mae grinned. "Thanks, Gal, you're pretty cool too."

Frankie shoved her bag at Mae. "Hold this my little feminist. I'm here and 'when in Rome'."

"Or Ljubljana."

"Exactly." Frankie crossed the bridge a couple of times, getting Bor to play photographer. Mae and Gal climbed up a balustrade to get a closer look at the dragons. Dina hung back with Ada. Hana knew damn well the dragon tails would wave for one of them, and not the other.

As for her. She didn't believe in the legend but still didn't want to risk some tail wagging at her expense. It was true. She was still a virgin. She'd never experienced more than one fumbling kiss with a family friend. She'd meet someone one day and it would happen, but she wanted to be in a relationship first. She knew she was old-fashioned but she made no apologies for that. It had never bothered her. It still didn't. But she didn't want any cheeky dragons making that public knowledge.

She could feel Drago beside her. She didn't dare look at him while they were near the bridge. She could feel him watching her.

"I haven't asked outright, but maybe I should… Do you have a boyfriend in Australia?"

"Why should you ask?" Hana finally looked up and challenged him with her eyes.

"Because I might have to kiss you while you're visiting, and I wouldn't do that if you were spoken for."

Hana's stomach back-flipped at the idea of him kissing her. She also liked the way he said, 'spoken for'. It was old-fashioned. "I'm not spoken for."

He smiled, an eyebrow raised. "I'm very pleased to hear that."

"I thought Mae told you that Dina is the only one with a boyfriend."

"I was just making sure."

Hana liked being with Drago. She liked getting to know him. His friends were fun. And Ljubljana was beautiful. Paris, her disappointment and dreams of it, drifted away while she enjoyed the night.

Bor jumped on Drago's back. "C'mon, let's go dragon hunting."

Mae and Gal joined them.

"Did I hear pizza?" Mae turned to Gal. "How do you say pizza in Slovenian?"

Gal gave her a serious look. "Pizza."

They both fell about laughing.

"I can't believe I'm older than you but you've finished school," Gal said to her. "You must be really smart."

Mae said. "I am, but so are you. I like you. And your English is good, Gal." She shot Bor a cheeky look. "So much better than

your brother's."

He laughed at that, clearly delighted by her. "I'm the family favourite. I went to an international school, while Bor went to the local school."

Bor ruffled his brother's head. "That's because you were expelled, you loser."

Mae raised her eyebrows. "You were?"

Gal nodded. "I organised a rally to challenge the government on some issues I believe in. The school didn't approve."

"I'm impressed."

Drago gathered the group together. "Okay, we can have pizza… but not yet. First up, we have organised a surprise for you girls. A very traditional Slovenian experience."

Mae and Frankie were clearly excited, while the other three held back until they knew more.

"I promise, you'll have fun." Drago said to Ada and was rewarded with a smile.

"Where to?" asked Mae, holding one arm up as if holding a sword.

Gal did the same. "Upwards."

Drago nodded. "He's right. We're going up there." He pointed at the castle, lit up in the evening light.

"Onward we march!" Mae shouted, leading Gal and the rest of the gang towards the base of the castle.

Hana and Drago walked behind the others. She pulled her jacket tight around herself and rubbed her hands together. They were icy, despite the wool gloves she was wearing.

Without saying another word, Drago reached out and took her hand. They walked quietly, side by side, and Hana wasn't cold anymore.

CHAPTER

# Twenty

"I can see the whole world," Mae squealed.

"I can see your house from here," Ada laughed.

"I can see Paris. Look."

Hana smiled at Frankie but couldn't help but think she was having a dig. She wasn't going to let it get to her. The view was amazing from Ljubljana castle.

They'd walked through the Ljubljana Central Market, closed for the day, and Vodnik Square and headed up a path to the Castle Hill. The walk took about fifteen minutes, with the group stopping to look down at the old town at various points along the way.

The girls still hadn't been told what they were doing, just that what they were doing was at the castle.

"Are we ghost-hunting?" Mae was trying to guess.

"Another Christmas market?" asked Ada.

"You're going to lock us in the dungeon?" Frankie laughed.

Hana was happy to do anything. She was happy doing exactly what she was doing. She couldn't remember being happier. It was crazy. She was with her best friends, in a beautiful place, having fun with some really great guys, and holding hands with possibly the nicest one she'd ever met.

Tonight, in his black jeans and boots, a grey pea coat and beanie, he looked like he'd just stepped out of a billboard. He was gorgeous, and smart, and lovely. And his attention was solely on her.

It felt surreal.

There were more people around their own age arriving now. Some in groups, others in pairs. They entered a huge courtyard that was alight with lanterns and two large screens playing music and showing dragon faces, sniffing and snorting smoke.

"Is it some sort of event?" Hana asked Drago

Bor overheard and clapped his hands together. "She's good. She will help us win!"

"Win? Are we playing a game?" Mae asked.

Bor motioned for them to gather round. He was good-looking, with a sharp nose and high cheekbones. He'd been following Ada around like a lost pup all night, but she seemed pretty disinterested. "There is a big event here tonight. You girls are going to help us…" His voice rose for theatrical effect, "… slay the dragon."

Mae's face lit up. "A game?"

"It's part game part laser tag experience. It's like an escape room… with laser guns."

"You Slovenians know how to have fun," Frankie said.

"This event is one night only but you're right," Drago said.

Frankie high-fived Mae. "Cool! Love it."

"Tonight they have turned the whole castle into a puzzle."

Mae jumped up and down. "I'm so excited I could burst."

Gal joined her, caught up in her enthusiasm.

"So, what do we do?" asked Dina.

Bor took over explaining. "You must take part as a team, so we have signed up as four teams. We can decide who goes with who. We will be competing against about twenty other teams tonight to slay the dragon and find the castle treasure."

"What do we win?" Mae asked.

"The winning team gets 500 Euro. The other teams get eaten

or locked in the dungeon."

"Very cool idea, guys. Good choice."

Hana and Drago joined forces, while Dina went with Bor, Frankie with Ada, and Mae with Gal. Hana knew it would be hard to beat Mae. Her brain easily found the answer before other people had even finished reading the question. But Hana had played paintball before, which was surely close to laser tag, so perhaps had the upper hand there. Either way, running around a medieval castle at night, with Drago by her side, was just about the most exciting thing she'd ever done.

They lined up with all the other pairs and were handed vests, laughing at each other as they put them on. It was already fun. Then they each got a gun that shot laser rays and a torch.

A trumpet-sound blared out. A man walked out of the castle holding a lantern. He was wearing robes, like a wizard or druid. A hush fell over the courtyard and people turned to listen. As he spoke, Drago translated for the girls.

"Thousands of years ago, Jason of the Argonauts slew the dragon of Ljubljana… or so we were told. In fact, the dragon was locked in one of the castle crypts, under the spell of an evil Grand Wizard. To exact revenge on the city that expelled him, the Grand Wizard crafted his spell to hold the dragon only until one fateful night, when the dragon would wake and destroy the city in a fiery inferno. That night is tonight.

You must solve the riddle to discover the dragon's lair and find a way to slay the dragon! But beware. There are shadow soldiers in the castle tonight, determined to thwart your progress. Anyone you see who is not in your team is a shadow soldier and must be shot. You have one hour to complete the task or Ljubljana will burn to the ground."

"No pressure," Frankie joked.

Hana could feel her heart racing. Even though the castle was lit up, she could still feel the shadows of hundreds of years of history around them.

More people in ornate robes stepped out from those shadows and began to pass rolled up scrolls and keys to the participants. Drago took his and turned to the rest of the group. "When the bell sounds, we no longer know each other."

Hana turned to the other girls. "Nice knowing you, biatches."

"For the next hour, you mean nothing to us," Dina said in mock seriousness.

The other three nodded, trying not to laugh.

"I'm gonna take you down," Mae said. "No mercy."

"Just don't pee yourself in the dark of the castle," Dina said. "You know you're afraid of the dark."

"True," Mae laughed.

"Don't worry, you have me," Gal said.

A gong sounded across the courtyard. Couples scattered everywhere. Most teams sprinted for various castle entrances. Drago motioned for Hana to follow him, while their friends disappeared. He led Hana to a lantern, where they stood under the light.

"Before we make any move to enter the castle, let's look at the first clue."

Hana nodded. Adrenaline coursed through her veins. Her hands shook as she clutched her gun.

Drago unrolled the scroll and translated what was on it.

"You think you know what a dragon looks like, but this dragon will lay the foundation for an unexpected surprise. You know where a dragon should be chained, but this one is kept in a place within a place."

Hana and Drago looked at each other and burst out laughing.

"Any ideas?" She asked.

"Not one."

They laughed and reread the scroll.

Drago shrugged. "Perhaps we just start searching and shooting people."

"Excellent plan."

They scanned the courtyard. It was empty now. Drago pointed to the castle. "That's a main entrance, so let's go to another door."

Hana followed him around the corner of the castle where it was more dimly lit. Drago motioned for her to follow him, close to the wall and into an entrance.

They stood for a moment, allowing their eyes to adjust to the dark. Hana's didn't, so she switched on her torch.

"That's better," she said.

"Just keep it facing the ground so it doesn't attract Shadow Soldiers."

They ran through one corridor after another, passing stone stairwells and locked rooms, only to find more locked doors at the other end.

Drago turned and led her back in the direction they'd come from, but this time taking a left instead of right. Hana could hear footsteps, so pulled Drago's arm and they stopped. She put her finger to her lips and switched off the torch. A shaft of moonlight coming through a nearby window broke the darkness.

"Shhh."

Drago stepped back into an enclave, and drew her in.

"I like watching your finger on your lips," he whispered.

Hana's heart raced. Adrenaline pumped through her. Not just from the event, which was thrilling itself, but from how close Drago was. The way he stared at her in the dark.

His eyes bore down on her. This is it, she thought. The energy between them was thick. It was too intense. They had to…

And he kissed her. Just like that, his lips met hers and, despite the fervour of the night, it was the most beautiful, gentle kiss Hana could've ever imagined.

Their lips were soft against each other's. He pulled her close and she wrapped her arms around him, not wanting the kiss to end.

It didn't.

It went on, and on… and time slipped away. The castle melted from sight. The darkness drew around them, keeping their secret, allowing them to have this moment together.

A moment Hana would remember forever.

Finally, she drew back. Her legs were weak. Her eyes were glazed. His stare matched hers.

"You're incredible," he whispered.

"You are too."

"I'm so lucky I met you."

Suddenly, Hana was grateful for all the things that went wrong in Paris, as they led her to this moment. A perfect moment.

"Hey, there's a party tomorrow night that my parents are throwing. Will you come? With your friends of course."

Did he want his parents to meet her? "I'd love to come."

"Great. I'll send a driver to get you all. It'll be fun."

He kissed her again and then pulled her in for a hug, as if they now shared a wonderful, joyous secret. She giggled. It really was perfect. More perfect than she ever imagined her first kiss to be.

Okay, second.

But that other fumbling session wouldn't count. It couldn't count next to this.

This was the kiss she'd remember as her first proper kiss.

And it was perfect.

"Let's go win this thing," she whispered.

"Or watch Mae win it," Drago said.

"Same thing."

He linked his fingers through hers and they ran towards the light. Hana could hear noise in the distance. They were halfway up the stairs when the winners' horn blew.

"That was quick."

"Not that quick… we were kissing for ages. Plenty of time for someone to crack the code."

Hana felt flushed. "Still… ten bucks on it being Mae."

They made their way to the castle courtyard. The place was lit up. They saw Ada, Dina, Frankie and Bor at the front of the crowd, waving them over.

Up on the podium were the dragon slayers, and winners of the competition.

"Mae and Gal!" she called.

They gave her a wave. Mae's face was brighter than the courtyard lanterns. Hana made it to the group, hugging Ada then Dina and then Frankie. They were all laughing and cheering for Mae and Gal, who took the winners' envelope and then made their way off the podium together.

Mae and Gal joined their friends, waving the envelope in front of them.

"Pizza on us!"

"How did you work it out so quickly?" Hana said.

Frankie butted in. "Ada and I would've won but couldn't read the clues."

Drago gave her a friendly hug. "I'm so sorry. I didn't even think to translate your instructions. But you had fun?"

"Oh yeah, it was awesome. We had no idea what we were

doing, but that made it even funnier."

Ada agreed. "I couldn't stop laughing so there's no way we'd have won anyway."

Frankie unzipped her vest. "Did you guys get shot?"

Drago gave Hana a wink. "Right in the chest."

Hana turned to Mae. "So, what was the code?"

"You think you know what a dragon looks like, but this dragon will lay the foundation for an unexpected surprise. You know where a dragon should be chained, but this one is kept in a place within a place." Gal nodded at Mae.

Mae looked at everyone as if it were crystal clear.

Drago shrugged. "In the dungeon?"

Mae rolled her eyes. "How obvious. Lay the foundation. A place within a place? The dragon hadn't been born. It was still in its egg. And the egg was hidden in the foundation of the castle."

"And how did you kill it?"

"Smashed the egg before it hatched."

The others stared at her momentarily and then looked at each other.

"Nope, still don't get it."

"Me either."

"I'd never get that."

"I was destined to lose."

Gal chimed in. "I just nodded a lot and pretended to get it. But really, Mae had solved the riddle before we'd even left the courtyard. It took about ten minutes to work out which part of the foundation the egg was in, but after that we came back up here and hung out for a while before blowing the horn. We didn't want to ruin the night by making it too short."

Everyone started to laugh.

Gal shrugged. "Her brain is insane."

"So's my stomach," Mae said, waving the winner's envelope at her friends. "Let's eat."

Drago pointed in a different direction. "Let's get the funicular railway to the bottom."

"Deal!" Mae started running towards it. "Last one there's a rotten dragon's egg."

# CHAPTER Twenty-One

Hana woke to the sound of her brother's voice. She realised Dina was lying in bed talking to him.

"Which of these Slovenian guys was the hottest?" Ronin teased.

"Oh, shut up, I didn't find any of them hot," Dina giggled. "They were nice though."

Hana pulled her pillow over her head in a vain attempt to block their voices out.

"Look who's awake!" Dina said.

"Like I had a choice," Hana mumbled from under the pillow.

"It's after ten."

"Erghmfff."

Dina reached over and pulled the pillow off Hana's face and shoved her phone in its place. "Want to say hi to Ronin?"

Not really, thought Hana, but muttered a faint hello anyway.

"Hey, Han, how's Paris?" Ronin joked.

"Too soon," Hana moaned.

Dina continued to shove the phone at her until she took it and sat up, wiping her hair off her face with her spare hand.

"You'll have another shot at Paris," Ronin said.

"That should be the title of a romance novel."

Ronin laughed, which took the edge off some of the tension between them.

Hana looked at him now, properly, on the screen. It was the first time they'd spoken since he turned up at the airport in Tokyo. The distance between them had nothing to do with geography, and everything to do with the fact that they hadn't resolved the argument they'd had when she was in Japan.

"Can we talk about it?" Ronin said as if reading her mind.

Dina jumped off her bed and pulled on her jeans and sweater. "I'm going down to check out the breakfast buffet. I'll bring you something back if you want?" She disappeared out the door without waiting for an answer.

Hana felt set up.

But then, she'd made a pact with herself and the spirit of her grandmother while sitting in the goulash café that she would 'go with the flow' and not be so overwhelmed by things.

Resolving things with Frankie didn't quite go to plan, but they'd had an okay night last night. It's not like they were fighting, or openly hostile. There was just tension. That could be fixed.

Hana knew one of the things that had really cast a shadow over her trip so far was the argument she'd had with Ronin in Japan. Even though he'd surprised them and turned up at the airport (more to see Dina than her, admittedly), it still hadn't been settled. And it needed to be, because Ronin was her rock. Her protector. Her most important person. They'd always been exceptionally close and fighting with him tore her apart.

"Yes, it's time to talk," she said to him. She fluffed some pillows up and leant back on them, comfortable and ready to take however long they needed.

"Everything okay with you, Han?"

She didn't want to tell him about last night. In the past she would've shared, but now wasn't the time to tell him about how it was the most magical night of her life. How she'd had the perfect kiss. She didn't want to share that with anyone yet, and risk breaking the spell. She certainly couldn't share something so important with him while there was this elephant in the room between them.

"Things are fine," she managed.

"Paris sounded eventful."

"That's putting it mildly." She sighed. "It wasn't what I expected it to be."

"Your expectations were pretty high."

"True."

"How were your results?"

Hana paused. Oh, what the hell. If she couldn't tell Ronin, who could she tell? "They weren't what I expected either."

"I see."

"I won't get my first preference."

"Hana, you're so talented and amazing… it will work out." They stared at each other, down the phone. "Did Baba ever tell you the story about Confucius and the river?"

Hana burst out laughing. "I was just thinking about that story yesterday."

"I adapted myself to the water, I didn't fight it," Ronin said. 'Without thinking, I allowed myself to be shaped by it. Plunging into the swirl, I moved with the swirl, I came out with the swirl…"

Hana finished with him. "This is how I survived the river."

"Just go with it."

"Yep."

"Or build a raft."

Hana chuckled. "Good idea."

There was an uncomfortable pause. One of them was going to have to confront the issue.

Ronin decided it would be him.

“We can discuss this amicably.”

“I agree.”

“I’ve thought about it and I absolutely disagree with you. We can’t tell Mum.”

Okay, maybe this conversation wasn’t going to be amicable.

“Then I’ll tell her,” Hana said.

“We agreed to be united on this. We both have to agree or not.”

“No Ronin, I’d prefer to be united but if you’re going to block me from doing what is right, then I’ll have to deal with this without you.”

She watched Ronin run his hand through his hair, the way he did when he was stressed.

“Why won’t you support me?” Hana asked, trying to get to the bottom of what was bothering him most.

“It’s not good timing.”

“What do you mean, timing?”

“I’m at a crucial point with the race suits. Midori could make or break these suits for me.”

“Are you serious? You’d let Mum suffer for some stupid swimsuit?”

“That’s unfair. I’ve worked my guts out for these.”

“Work,” Hana snarled.

“This isn’t just about the tech suit line. It’s about paying Dad back. About winning his respect back. I owe him.”

“Stuff him. What about Mum?”

“I get why you’re so upset, Hana. And I am too… about that. But last time… when I sold the SkipBoard designs… Dad never even judged me. He kept business and family so separate.”

“Unlike when he had an affair with his assistant.”

“I’m talking about how he dealt with me. I wasn’t punished. Instead, he addressed his relationship with me. I owe him the same, to keep these things separate." He looked like he was going to cry but took a moment and it passed. "I get it. I get the anger. I get what he's done. Again. But he's still our father and we need to be careful."

"You be careful with Dad. I'll be loyal to Mum."

Ronin glared at her. "Okay, you need to do what you feel is right. When will you tell her?"

Hana shrugged. "I don't know. I need to think it through now I'm on my own with this. I hate the idea of calling from Slovenia and saying, 'Oh, by the way, your life is a lie… sorry you're alone to deal with it'."

"Will you wait until you get home?"

"Maybe. But that's weeks away."

"Speak to Dina about it."

"Right, talk to your girlfriend about our fight." Hana knew that was unfair, the moment it came out her mouth. Dina didn't take sides. She was objective and gave really good advice. "Yes, I'll talk to her."

"I've gotta go." Ronin stared at his sister. "I'm sorry I can't give you what you want."

"Ronin, just think about what Mum would want."

"Guilt won't work. There's more at stake for me than you."

"That's such crap. The only person with anything at stake is Mum and she doesn't know because you're too stubborn to tell her."

Ronin looked furious but calmed and said. "Enjoy your trip."

And with that he hung up.

Hana stared at the screen for a moment, feeling her anger build. She was tempted to smash the phone against the wall, but knew she'd regret it later.

Instead, she buried her head in a pillow and screamed.

# CHAPTER Twenty-Two

The door opened slightly and an arm holding a plate of fruit, breads and cheeses appeared. "Peace offering," came Dina's voice, before she stuck her head through.

Hana wiped the tears from her eyes and gave her a wry smile. "You're lucky you brought food, after what you did to me."

Dina entered and closed the door behind her. "You had to talk to him at some stage," she said, sitting at the foot of Hana's bed. "Here, eat."

Hana took the plate.

"Clearly it didn't go well."

"No, your boyfriend is a stubborn pain in the butt."

"Tell me something I don't know."

Hana cracked a smile. She couldn't help it. Dina was good value and didn't fawn over Ronin.

"You didn't resolve things?" Dina asked.

"Made them worse. We just don't see eye to eye on this… issue. And it's really tough. I mean, the issue is tough enough… but I've always had Ronin's support. In everything. We're peas in a pod."

Dina smiled. "That's what Mae and I call ourselves."

"Really? Then you get it. You're different… wildly different, but there's that bond. Loyalty."

"You still have that with him."

"It doesn't feel like I do. For now, I'm alone."

"No, you have me," Dina took a fig off the plate. "Tell me

what's going on. What's this all about?"

Hana sighed. "Dad's having an affair."

"Another one?"

"Yes, another one."

"Same woman?"

"No. Different one."

"Are you sure?"

Hana nodded. "Remember when you were at the beach house with Ronin and you came out wearing a robe?"

"Of course. His mood completely changed. It ruined the last bit of our getaway."

"It had the name of a woman on it," Hana explained.

"I figured it belonged to your grandmother and I'd made a dreadful faux pas wearing it."

"No, not at all. It had nothing to do with anything you did. I'm sorry he didn't make that clear. If anything, you putting it on did us a favour, because now we know."

"Do you know the woman?" Dina asked.

"Yes. And so do you. It's Midori."

Dina stared at Hana, shocked. "Mean Midori? Midori who works at Hi Ho? You can't be serious."

"One hundred per cent."

Dina thought about it for a moment. "I guess it makes sense. She really doesn't belong at Hi Ho. She doesn't fit in at all, and yet she's there, making trouble for Ronin."

"Yep."

"We had one meeting with her and she was a bit of a bitch," Dina said. "No wonder he was so upset. But why did you two fight?"

"Because he won't tell Mum."

"Maybe he doesn't want to hurt her?"

"Actually, he said he's too close to making a breakthrough with the tech suits and doesn't want to risk Midori stuffing things up for him."

This clearly surprised Dina. "Wow, okay… not cool."

"Right. That's what I think. Although I'm surprised you agree with me."

"Why? It's the right position to take here. Just because he's my boyfriend doesn't mean I'm going to pander to him, especially if he's wrong about something important."

"Sorry, you're right," Hana said. "That's not you."

"I absolutely understand why he's thinking like this. It's about your dad and that board drama? When he stole the designs?"

"Correct."

"Damn him and his issues about not mixing business and personal… although clearly your father does too much of that." Dina punched Hana lightly on the arm. "I'm joking."

"I know. It would be funny, if it wasn't so heartbreaking."

"Your mum has no idea?"

"Not that I'm aware of. She's so happy again. They've been like newlyweds for the past year."

"Ouch."

Hana jumped off the bed signalling the end of the topic. She decided to push the conversation with Ronin to the back of her mind. It was yet another thing on her 'deal with that later' list. Along with Frankie, her HSC results and Paris.

"What's the plan today?"

Dina shrugged. "Frankie is going to the Slovenian Tourist Board. They've arranged a photographer and some free activities or something. She asked if we wanted to come but Ada and Mae said they wanted to chill."

"I'm with them," Hana said. "And we've got that party

tonight. I need to work out what to wear." The thought of meeting Drago's family and friends made her nervous. She wanted to make the right impression.

There was a knock on the door. "Room service," came Frankie's voice.

Dina opened the door and Frankie breezed in.

"Your fairy godmother has arrived," she announced.

"I thought the fairy godmother was spending the day with the tourist board."

"True, I am… but I also have a bit of a surprise." She handed Hana a piece of paper with an address on it. "We all have to be at this address at four."

"What for?"

"Four pm." Frankie chuckled at her joke. "I know what you mean. Anyway, seeing as none of us have suitable cocktail dresses in our backpacks, I made a call to a local designer and we're all going to be dressed for tonight."

Dina's face lit up. "Are you serious? I was dreading wearing jeans."

"What's the catch?" asked Hana.

"We just need to post some shots on Insta in the clothes."

"Who's the designer?"

"Vesna Vidmar."

"I think I've heard of her." Hana grabbed her phone, now thankful she didn't smash it, and quickly Googled the designer. "Oh wow, yes, her stuff is beautiful."

Frankie gave Hana a strange look. "So, that's a yes?"

Hana thought about Drago. And the kiss. She hadn't stopped thinking about it. And tonight she was going to his family home. She'd meet his family and friends. She wanted to look amazing.

"Yes, that's great." Hana gave the girls an eye roll. "I know, I know… I'm a hypocrite."

Frankie laughed. "But you want to look good for Drago. I want you to look good for Drago."

Hana walked over to Frankie and gave her a hug. She did truly love her friend, and really appreciated her doing this for her. Frankie looked like a child, she was so happy to have Hana back on side.

"I've got to go, but I'll see you all at the showroom at four." Frankie disappeared out the door.

Hana gave Dina a wink and threw herself on the bed, arms splayed.

She'd made up with her friend and it felt great.

Some things were even better than kissing a gorgeous guy.

# CHAPTER Twenty-Three

"I have hit the jackpot."

The girls stood huddled together while a man called Blazhe snapped pictures of them.

"You are all so beautiful; I cannot believe my massive jackpot."

Mae and Ada began to giggle, only to receive a sharp elbow from Frankie, which made them laugh harder.

Hana, Dina, Mae and Ada had arrived at the showroom at four to find Frankie already there, having drinks with Vesna, the designer, a photographer Vesna had hired and a gorgeous young woman around their own age.

Vesna was a stylish brunette with a striking streak of grey in her hair. She had greeted the girls warmly.

"I'm so happy you're going to wear my designs to this party." She glanced at Hana. "You know the Lazar family is very well known in this country, so there will be many famous and important people there."

Hana could feel the nerves hit. She was no social slouch. Her parents often partied with well-known people, but usually they were famous surfers or musicians and other celebrity Hi Ho devotees.

Vesna turned and introduced the girl. "This is my goddaughter, Zoe. She's visiting from London."

Zoe was something else. Her tight black curls were styled on top with purple streaks running through them, and the sides were shaved short. She wore high-waisted deep green pants, and a striped shirt. She held up a sketchpad and smiled at the girls. "I hope you don't mind me making some sketches while Vesna styles you."

They all agreed it was fine. They would have agreed if she'd said,' I hope you don't mind but I'm going to spray you with cat urine'. Zoe gave off the kind of cool vibe where you'd agree to anything with her.

Vesna took over again. "And this is Blazhe. He will take some photos of you for Frankie's accounts."

"How do I pronounce your name?" Mae asked the question the others wanted to ask.

"Blaz heeee," he said.

The girls all tried it a few times until he said they were geniuses as well as super models.

"I'm still getting the hang of Slovenian names," Hana explained to him, thinking of Drago.

Blazhe waved a hand in front of his face. "No, darling, I'm not Slovenian. I'm Macedonian."

"Next to Greece?" Frankie said.

His eyes widened in horror. "Please don't ever utter that word around me again." And then he smiled and gathered the girls into a group and through a door to a studio where his camera gear was set up.

"What was that about?" Dina whispered to the others.

"North Macedonia and Greece haven't been the friendliest neighbours," Mae explained. "There has been an ongoing argument over the name, Macedonia, until recently when Macedonia adopted a North onto theirs. It helped ease tensions."

"I shouldn't have said anything," Frankie said.

"I think he was joking," Mae said. "But still, don't mention

Alexander the Great."

"How do you know these things?" Dina asked.

Mae shrugged. "How do you not?"

The first round of photos was of the girls dressed in the gear they'd arrived in. Hana and Frankie were both in skirts and boots. Mae wore her usual overalls, and Dina and Ada rocked their jeans. They all looked casual and cool, although Hana noticed some scuffing and fraying of clothes after weeks of wearing the same outfits.

The girls were asked to stand in front of a white backdrop. There was an old A-frame ladder, and a box on the floor in front.

"Just be yourselves, and be fabulous," Blazhe said, picking up his camera.

Themselves and fabulous were a little uncomfortable. The first few clicks of the camera were awkward, until Frankie, who clearly had some practice posing, jumped into a bold, large pose, which cracked the others up and broke the ice. After that, they had some fun, with a range of positions. Arms draped over each other. Some girls sitting, while others stood. Frankie climbed to the top of the ladder. Mae star-jumped in front of them all and acted like such a clown they all couldn't stop laughing. Even Zoe, who was seated in the corner scribbling on her sketchpad.

"Beautiful!" Blazhe yelled. "Wonderful. So good I could cry. You are like… traveller girls."

"Gypsy girls." Frankie responded.

"Actually, the word 'gypsy' is derogatory," Mae said. "So, you need to stop using it in hashtags."

"But it's a great word," Frankie said.

"It reinforces racist stereotypes of Romani people, especially women."

"It's true," came Zoe's voice from the back of the room.

Frankie stared at Mae and then over at Zoe. "Seriously? I had no idea."

"Most people don't. But once you know, you need to change your relationship with the word." Mae shrugged.

Hana marvelled at Mae. One moment she was a complete clown, the next she was the smartest person she knew. Maybe the two went hand-in-hand. Hana understood the complexities of race and identity. In Australia, she was often asked where she came from. "I'm Australian," she'd respond. "Yes, but where are you from... you know, before that."

Japan was worse. Japanese people often made it obvious she wasn't one of them, even though she identified with her Japanese-ness. But how she identified didn't count... It's how others identified her.

She'd spent a lot of time in Japan, but never enjoyed it as much as this recent trip with her friends. Seeing how much they loved Japan, especially Dina's deep connection to the place (not to mention Hana's brother) meant that Hana had experienced Japan through fresh eyes. Instead of being the mixed-race kid, struggling to have the Japanese part of her identity recognised as valid, she was able to move beyond that and share stories about her grandparents with her friends, and things about Japanese culture that she loved. It helped her accept her identity more. Not just accept it, because she'd always accepted being half Japanese... more than that. She held it up and said, 'I don't care if you don't think I'm Japanese enough; I do identify as this'.

"Okay, so scrap that word," Frankie said. "No more of those hashtags. So what do I call us when I post these?"

"Wander girls?" Blazhe said.

"Holiday girls?" Vesna chimed in.

"Travel girls?"

"Backpacker crew?"

Zoe's voice called out from the back. "You are the lost girls!"

And all five girls looked at each other. It was perfect.

"Come on, lost girls," said Vesna. "Time to get dressed up."

CHAPTER

# Twenty-Four

Hana

Dina

Mae

Frankie

Ada

CHAPTER

# Twenty-Five

"These are amazing," Hana said as she flicked through Zoe's sketchbook. There were pages of sketches she'd made of the girls that afternoon. "Are you a designer?"

"Student. I'm studying Fashion Imaging and Illustration at the London College of Fashion."

'Very cool. I want to study design too," Hana admitted.

"Fashion?"

"Interior."

Zoe nodded, as if they were both part of the same special club. "I was always inspired by Vesna. She lived in London for years, then when she brought the label back to be based here, I was old enough to come over and spend holidays with her. I'm still not sure exactly what I specifically want to do, but this is the world."

Mae entered the room looking sensational in a satin tuxedo. It was dressy, but also suited her perfectly. Each of the girls had been dressed by Vesna, and then had their hair and makeup done, before Blazhe took their photo together as a group. Then one by one they had some individual shots done and signed a waiver saying they could be used across social media and marketing for both Frankie and Vesna's brands.

Hana finished first and had joined Zoe at the back of the room.

Mae perched herself on the bench on the other side of Zoe. "Where in London are you?"

"Camden. Do you know it?"

"Not yet, but we're going to London."

"Last stop on this trip," Hana said.

"I can't wait to get there," Mae said. "I've always wanted to go to London. I plan to live there."

Hana didn't know this about her friend. "Really? When?"

Mae shrugged. "Soon."

"After uni?"

"Something like that." Mae looked at the notebook Zoe was holding. "Is that me?"

Zoe showed her. "It is… you look great. How old are you?"

"Sixteen."

"And you've finished school and are travelling alone?"

"No, I have my friends." Mae pointed at Dina who was having her turn in front of the camera, in a black cocktail dress. "That's my older sister. My parents roped her into chaperoning."

"Are you gifted?"

Mae rolled her eyes. "Whatever that means."

Zoe nodded. "Yes, I'm apparently gifted too. Assessed at nine, off the charts IQ, but can't write because I have dysgraphia."

"You're 2E?" Mae said.

"Yes."

"What's 2E," Hana asked.

"Another ridiculous label," Zoe laughed. "Twice exceptional, meaning gifted, but with a learning issue that masks that."

"And dys— what was it?"

"Dysgraphia. Means I can't get the stuff that's in my head onto paper. Writing is tough. Just another label." Zoe paused then started ticking them off with her fingers as she continued. "As well as being a black, half-Slovenian, lesbian woman. It's just another to add to the list."

"I know all about labels. I hate them," Mae said.

"What are your labels?" Zoe asked Hana.

"I don't know. Asian. That's in Australia. In Japan it's hafu. Meaning half."

"What if you're half Japanese but born and raised in Japan. You're Japanese then, right?" Zoe asked.

"No, still hafu. You don't get to identify as Japanese apparently."

Zoe rolled her eyes. "Wow."

Mae pointed at Ada. "She's got all sorts of labels attached to her as well."

"The supermodel?"

"Yeah, but that's the worst one. She hates being defined by her looks."

"I get that." Zoe grinned at the girls. "Let's swap details and catch up when you're in London. I can show my label girls around."

Mae slapped her legs with her hands as if she'd just heard the funniest thing ever. "Label girls, love it."

Hana cracked up too. "Funny. But I like the lost girls better."

CHAPTER

# Twenty-Six

The girls fell silent as the van pulled into a driveway and paused at a wrought iron gate. A few moments later, the gate opened, and they drove down a private road until the villa appeared.

"He calls that thing a villa?" Frankie said.

"Wow," Mae said. "Glad I didn't wear my boots."

Hana's eyes widened. "Oh, Frankie, thank god you scored these dresses for us."

"Whatever, it's similar to my place," Ada joked. She and her mother lived in a tiny two-bedroom apartment.

The villa was actually a three-story contemporary style mansion with sprawling gardens. It was shaped like three cubes placed on top of each other and made of brick and glass.

The driver rang the doorbell for them and then returned to the van.

"What would you do if a zombie answered?" Mae said.

"Seriously? You ask that right now?" Hana gave her a zip-it glare.

A woman in a nicely cut but rather uninspiring skirt and jacket opened the door.

Hana stepped forward and shook her hand. "Hello, Mrs Lazar. I'm Hana Honda. Drago invited us."

"Very good. The family is gathered downstairs. Let me show you the way." The woman withdrew her hand and smiled politely. "And you can meet Mrs Lazar there."

Mae and Frankie cracked up, which also set Dina and Ada off.

"You thought the maid was his mother," Mae whispered.

"Oh shut up!" Hana hissed.

The woman led them inside, and that's where the full impact of Drago's family home hit them. The entry was on the second floor, which led to a view of both the floors above and below. Above, the third floor appeared to be fronted in glass, and looking up Hana could see the night sky in some parts of the house. Looking down, the view was straight onto a massive entertaining and living area. Dozens of well-dressed people were milling around in groups, cocktails in hand. The open living and dining space spilled out glass doors onto a terrace that was lit up with designer lights and surrounded by a number of open fire pits.

They passed three bedrooms and what appeared to be a home theatre. Making their way down a winding staircase, Hana noticed a walkway to the right, leading to a glassed area with an indoor pool. Despite the open plan, the house was warm, with heated marble floors and open fireplaces. At the side of the stairs, there was a glass elevator, connecting all the floors.

"Holy batman," Mae mumbled.

As they reached the foot of the stairs, Hana spotted Drago in the crowd. He was dressed in a navy suit and pale blue shirt, with brown belt and shoes. He wasn't wearing a tie. Instead his shirt was casually unbuttoned three from the top and his jacket hung open. Hana's pulse sped up. She experienced a full physical reaction to seeing him that included butterflies in her stomach and a slight weakening of the knees. Usually contained, Hana noticed how she felt and marvelled that so many stupid romance novels could actually be right.

He turned and their eyes locked across the room. There was a moment of sheer intensity as he acknowledged her gaze, and then his face lit up. He was obviously delighted to see her, and all her nerves disappeared in an instant. Without another word to the people he was talking to, he marched straight across the room to Hana.

"You're here," he said as he arrived beside her.

"I'm here," she answered. Cheesy yes, but it felt great.

Drago gave her a hug and then greeted the rest of the girls. Hana spotted Bor and Gal across the room and gave them a wave. This wasn't so bad.

Suddenly an attractive woman with a rather taut face appeared before her. She had the same hooded dark eyes and high cheekbones as Drago.

"Welcome, girls, I'm Irina."

Drago smiled as he welcomed his mother into the circle they'd formed. "Mother, this is Hana."

Hana watched as Irina's smile froze… or perhaps she was jumping to conclusions and that was just her face.

"Hello, Hana. Thank you for coming to our party."

She turned her back on Hana and greeted the other girls, one by one, more warmly, until her gaze rested on Frankie and she broke into the first genuine smile.

"I know who you are. I've been following your Instagram since Drago said he met you in Paris."

That even surprised Frankie. "You have Instagram?"

"Of course. How old do you think I am?"

"Mum heads up our hotel PR division," Drago explained.

"We've found Instagram to be a marvellous way to reach younger travellers who can afford a nice hotel," she said, "So we are very pleased you were able to take up the offer of staying with us. Especially after such a shocking experience in Paris."

Hana watched on, mortified. Frankie had rolled with the punches in Paris. She was the one who'd been traumatised, not Frankie. Irina wasn't finished yet.

"I see you posted from the hotel pool, which I appreciate. A very clever use of lighting and space. You have a real gift. Perhaps you can add another couple of posts while you're here?"

Hana felt the floor shift beneath her. Were they here because of Frankie? Had Drago invited them to Slovenia because of Frankie's stupid Instagram account?

Was it Frankie he'd been interested in and not her?

She actually felt off-balance, as if the scene she was in wasn't real, but rather some weird virtual reality. She blinked a couple of times, but nothing shifted. She was still watching Drago's mother warmly welcome Frankie, while completely ignoring her. And Drago stood beside her smiling, as if that were perfectly acceptable.

Some new guests had arrived and were making their way down the stairs. Irina turned to Drago and said something in Slovenian, and then one final sunbeam smile at Frankie. "I must greet our guests. We'll talk more later."

Drago gave Hana a wink, as if he hadn't witnessed the same scene as her and followed his mother to the foot of the stairs.

"What the hell was that?" Dina was the first to speak.

The girls took a few steps towards Hana, creating a huddle around her.

"She must know you and Drago are getting it on," Mae said.

"One kiss hardly means we're getting it on," Hana said. "Maybe she doesn't like Asians. I've noticed there aren't many in Ljubljana."

But Hana knew it wasn't that. Or wasn't only that. Drago's

mother was a businesswoman and was interested in the power of Frankie's social media reach. It was easy advertising for the boutique hotel.

"That was awkward," Frankie said.

Hana glared at her friend. "For you or for me?"

"For both of us."

"Why was it awkward for you?"

"Because I didn't ask for that. Because you're my friend. Or at least you used to be." And with that Frankie walked off towards Bor and Gal.

"I understand that you're hurt and confused," Ada said, "but that wasn't Frankie's fault".

Mae and Ada followed Frankie across the room.

"I feel like battle lines have been drawn," Dina joked. "Where do I stand?"

"Well, Mae is your sister," Hana said.

"But I'm dating your brother... so either way I'm stuffed."

Hana managed a weak smile. "I know they're right. I know Frankie didn't ask for this. I'm just so sick of her obsession with her account."

"Not sick enough of it to turn down that dress you're wearing."

"I know. I get that I'm a hypocrite."

"You look amazing by the way."

"You do too." Hana whispered her greatest worry. "What if he only invited us here because of Frankie's Instagram?"

"There's only one way to find out."

"How's that?"

Dina rolled her eyes at her friend. "Ask him."

CHAPTER

# Twenty-Seven

Hana stood at the edge of the garden, shivering. The party had livened up as the champagne flowed, with louder music and louder people. Everyone spilled onto the terrace behind her. She'd spent the past two hours chatting politely to strangers, all of whom were interested in her and where she came from. Unlike Drago's mother, who had appeared again to drag Frankie away for a fabulous photo opportunity.

Frankie obliged, but Hana noticed it was with some trepidation and a nervous glance at her.

She still went.

Hana had grown up in a wealthy family, but even this was too much. It wasn't the money as much as how out of place she felt, because she clearly wasn't of importance.

Certainly not to Drago's mother.

Perhaps not to Drago.

And that stung, because she'd let her guard down with him, and had developed real feelings for him. She knew it was fast, and early, but it was real. To her. She'd never experienced anything like it. She'd never experienced anything more than a passing crush here and there. But even those boys didn't keep her attention very long. They always seemed so… young.

Not Drago. He was mature. And it was that maturity that appealed to her, even more than the tall, muscular physique, or brooding eyes, or full lips. Although those things were all extremely appealing too. But it was his steadiness. She enjoyed his company and felt secure with him. She didn't want one of those crazy, wild relationships that other girls her age craved. She didn't want drama.

Was she getting it without realising? What did she really know about him? Nothing. She'd stupidly believed that he'd invited them here because he was kind, and perhaps interested in her. But clearly he'd seen Frankie's Instagram and thought it was a smart business move.

Which made Hana feel rather stupid.

"I've been looking for you."

Hana felt something warm cover her shoulders and realised it was one of the cashmere throws that were scattered around on the outdoor lounges. She pulled it tight around her shoulders, grateful for the warmth.

"You don't like the party?" Drago took her by the arm and gently turned her so they were facing each other. "Are you okay?"

"I'm fine," she said. "I'm just admiring your garden. And the view." She motioned at the lights of Ljubljana that twinkled in the distance.

"I would like to take you to Lake Bled for a couple of nights."

Hana was thrown by the wording of that. Just her? "Do you mean all of us?"

"Of course, you, Frankie… all the girls."

Hana bristled. Frankie. "What's in Lake Bled?"

"It's a very beautiful spot, so you must see it while you are in Slovenia." He reached out and pushed a lock of hair off her face. "Also, the place I call my hotel is there. I would like you to see it."

His hotel. He said it with a certainty that Hana recognised. She often said similar things to herself, if she saw a bag, or pair of shoes she liked. She'd say 'my shoes' even before she bought them, but a hotel was in a completely different league altogether.

"I'd like that," Hana said. But she also needed to know if he wanted her to see it… or wanted it featured on Frankie's Instagram.

They faced each other, their breath coming out in clouds.

She needed to ask him. Just confront it. Hana took a deep breath. She wasn't good with confrontation. Ronin, Frankie, now Drago… Hana had a tendency to let things slide, or fester, rather than directly address and resolve. She wanted resolution, but in the moment the courage often eluded her.

"Drago…"

"Yes."

She had his full attention. The way he gazed straight into her eyes, and beyond. His mind wasn't back on the party, or anywhere else, he really was present for her.

And just as she went to open her mouth to speak, it began to snow.

Really snow.

Large flakes fell from the sky, melting as they landed on them. Hana and Drago both looked up at the heavens and then back at each other, huge smiles lighting their faces. They began to laugh, looking up, and then at each other, over and over again. Until in one joyous moment Drago pulled Hana towards him, and his lips landed on hers. She slid her arms around his neck and melted into him, as if she too was a snowflake.

She forgot the cold.

She forgot the snow.

She forgot where she was.

She forgot to ask why he'd invited them all to visit Slovenia.

# CHAPTER Twenty-Eight

"The wheels on the bus go round and round, round and round…"

Apparently Bor and Gal had lived in London for a few years when they were younger, so knew the lyrics to one of the world's most annoying songs when Mae started singing it.

When Drago mentioned his plans to visit Bled with the girls, Gal and Bor announced they'd come too. So, Drago arranged a mini bus, and Hana found herself squished beside Drago (no problem there) hurtling along the highway out of the city. Everyone was chatting and laughing and singing stupid songs. Frankie hadn't spoken to Hana since the party the night before, although the tension with Ada and Mae had passed by morning.

On the way, they stopped in Škofja Loka.

"You must see it," Drago said. "It's one of Slovenia's oldest and most lovely towns."

He was right. They wandered around the medieval streets, from one small town square, up cobblestone streets to a larger one circled by colourful old houses. It was wonderful having the guys with them on this part of the trip. Obviously, Hana had good reasons to want Drago around, but her friends appeared to like him a lot too now. As to the brothers, while Bor had stuck his foot in his mouth that first night at the Dragon Bridge, he was actually kind and funny. Gal was too, but also cut from the same clown-like cloth as Mae.

After Škofja Loka, they continued on to Bled via a scenic

drive up through the mountains and past places with names like Jamnik and Kropa.

Hana was glued to the window, absorbing all she could about this delightful country. The traffic got heavier as they drove into Bled. The sky was a vibrant blue and from the warmth of the car she could almost kid herself that it was summer. But the trees they passed were bare, and the children running along the footpath wore winter coats and boots.

They drove through a roundabout, taking the opposite direction they would in Australia, a reminder of how she could never drive here. Petrol stations, rambling guesthouses, nothing special really. And then she spotted it. They all did. Lake Bled. It was only a glimpse of it and Drago assured them that the best was still to come, but the girls gasped and pointed when they saw the colour of the water.

"Lake Bled has been spared from pollution because motorised boats are banned," Drago explained.

"I see some boats on there now," Hana said.

"Those are called pletna. And they are row boats. They don't use fossil fuel."

They turned off the main road and drove through a few streets with small hotels and cafés, before turning again and heading into a forested area.

Hana was looking forward to seeing 'Drago's dream hotel' as he'd called it earlier. After seeing the hotel in Ljubljana and then his family home, she was certain they were in for a modern, but stylish boutique hotel.

They turned onto a gravel drive. Hana saw glimpses of the lake through the trees that suggested they were driving towards it.

"We're very fortunate to be on seven acres here. So close to

Bled, but still rather isolated."

Isolated was putting it mildly. It was a thick forest. Hana half expected to spot wolves or bears.

"It's just up ahead," Drago said.

The other girls fell silent in the back. Hana craned her neck to get a look.

They emerged from the trees, and a chateau stood in a small clearing at the edge of the lake.

Only it wasn't modern.

Or anything like what Hana expected.

Mae voiced what the others were thinking. "Holy hell, it looks like something from a horror movie."

# CHAPTER Twenty-Nine

Even close up in the sunlight, it looked like it housed a family of vampires.

The house was a very old, four-story, traditional villa, with peeling paint, and crumbling stone. It was set on an elevated position above the lake and surrounded by a lush green garden.

Hana glanced at Drago. He was beaming, obviously happy to see the place.

"I know it doesn't seem like the best hotel in Europe now, but one day it will be."

"Until then, it sucks the souls of everyone that enters its doors," Mae said dramatically.

Drago laughed. At least he thought Mae was being funny.

They followed Drago into the villa and Hana was surprised to see that it looked lived in, as if it was someone's home. Old, heavy furniture filled the maze of rooms. Fraying rugs covered the wooden floors. Framed photos lined the mantles of the ceramic fireplaces. Two of them, one in the kitchen and one in a lounge, quickly fired up when Drago lit them.

Drago led everyone up a flight of heavy wooden stairs and down a long, dark corridor.

"You can have any of these rooms," he said opening three doors as he passed. One had two single beds, the next had a double bed, while the final, smaller room housed a single. All the rooms had adjoining bathrooms and balconies.

Mae took charge. "Frankie and Ada have the singles. I'll

sleep with Dina in the double bed. Safety in numbers and all that. Hana is the only one of us who can watch a horror film without flinching, so she gets the single room to herself."

Dina looked at Hana. "You okay with that?"

Hana was okay, for all sorts of reasons. She could do with some time out from the others. One reason was she didn't know where things were heading with Drago, so a room to herself would be convenient if anything happened. But mainly, she'd had overload with all the recent tension with her friends. A room to herself, where she could retreat if necessary, sounded ideal.

Drago and the brothers continued on to the next floor up while Hana dragged her case into her bedroom. The bed was covered in a beautiful, but faded, patchwork quilt. It had a lovely bedside table with a lamp on it, a writing desk under one window, and French doors leading to a covered balcony with ornate wooden lattice.

She flopped down on the bed and took a deep breath. She'd gone off alone in Ljubljana, which had been great, but this was the first time since leaving Australia that she'd actually been alone. In a room alone. It was nice. And looking around the room at that moment, at the elegant details, the stained glass in one window, the antique doorknobs, Hana realised that Drago was right. This place had huge potential as a hotel. But what was it now? A holiday home?

Her eyes drifted to the view beyond her balcony. She climbed off the bed and went outside to have a look. Spectacular was not a word that did it justice. The forest below, the lake in front and then mountains in the distance.

She shook her head in disbelief, completely moved by the view, and immediately recognised how that feeling had been missing in Paris. What was it about Slovenia? The surprise of it?

The people she had met? The things she'd experienced?

She was more relaxed here and perhaps that was a part of it. She liked who she was here more. Drago made her feel special, which was exciting for her. But Hana knew it ran deeper than just pinning everything on how a guy felt about her. She'd stepped outside her comfort zone here, by choice. She'd tried new things. She'd embraced some time alone. She hadn't let her issues with Frankie or Ronin or her father get in the way. She wasn't dwelling too much on her HSC marks.

Hana felt her strength start to show in Slovenia, and she liked that.

Dina stuck her head in the room. "Hey, we're going to go down to the lake. Coming?"

Hana smiled. "Wouldn't miss it."

Mae's voice echoed through her door. "Also wouldn't want to be left at Dracula's castle alone."

Hana laughed. "I don't believe in vampires."

"Yeah, yeah." Mae stuck her head into the room, with a grin. "Give it a night, and you'll be begging me for a garlic necklace."

CHAPTER

# Thirty

The lake was quite possibly the most incredible thing Hana had ever seen. Shimmering blue, so clear you could see to the very depths of it. The group had left the house and walked through the forest to the water's edge, where they made their way around the lake on a path. The closer they got to town, the more built up it was, with a range of hotels from beautiful villas to dated resorts. The town of Bled was in the distance. High above it all on a cliff top was Bled Castle. Looking back in the direction they'd come was more forested land, with the occasional rooftop poking through the trees. And then, in the centre of the lake, was the tiny jewel of Bled Island, jutting up out of the water, a church on top.

Drago led them to a boatshed and received a warm welcome from the old man working there. They spoke in Slovenian for a while and then Drago turned and introduced him to the others in English.

"This is Ivan. He is a master boatbuilder. We're going to take some of his rowboats onto the lake."

"Are they like the ones over there?" Mae asked, pointing to a number of boats with a cover across the top, holding about a dozen people.

"No, those are the pletna. And usually the owner of the boat rows it. Tourists ride those. These are rowboats. And we row."

Drago gestured to some boats lined along the shore. All were carved by hand from a caramel coloured wood.

"I don't see any life jackets," Ada said.

"I'll sit with you," Dina said.

Ada visibly relaxed, obviously comfortable having one of Australia's top swimmers by her side if the boat sank.

A few minutes later, Hana found herself in one rowboat with Drago, Gal and Mae. The others were in a second boat. Ivan used his foot to push the boats into the water and then with Bor and Drago rowing the boats, they floated out onto the lake and towards the island.

It was a cold day, but the air was crisp and clean and the skies a vibrant blue that matched the water. There was a serene stillness and silence on the lake, apart from the gentle splash of oars. Hana soaked in the view. It was absolutely stunning. Once again, she was feeling incredibly happy. She knew Drago played a part in that. She was really enjoying her time with him and didn't like to consider what would happen when she left. That was also one reason she hadn't confronted him about his mother's reaction to Frankie—she really didn't want to ruin this feeling. Or their few days together. But she would ask. She needed to know. When the time was right. In the meantime, she was just happy to be around him, in this wonderful place.

Mae was the one to break the spell, moving over towards Drago.

"Can I have a go rowing?"

"Of course." He handed her the oars and swapped seats, being careful not to rock the boat too much.

Mae wrapped her tiny hands around the large oars and began to push them through the water. The boat began to turn. Hana watched her friend pull some funny faces as she tried to right the direction of the boat. She pulled one row up, and then the other, but the boat began to move in a circle.

Hana and Drago began to laugh.

Mae followed.

Gal lay back and joked, "This could take some time. Wake me when we're there."

Which made them all laugh more.

"Clearly Dina got the sporty gene," Hana said, almost crying she was laughing so hard.

The boat continued to spin. Mae pulled herself together and had a look of pure focus on her face. "I can't believe it's so hard." And with that, something clicked, and she eased the boat into a stable position, and they began to move towards the island again.

"Never underestimate me," Mae said.

"The others are almost there," Hana said.

"That's Ada's fear of sinking that's driving the boat," Mae giggled.

Hana looked ahead at the island. "Do people live there?"

"No, it has always been a place of worship, starting with the..." Drago searched for the word. "Pre-Christian people."

"Pagans?" Mae offered.

"Yes. Them. The current church is from the seventeenth century, but archaeologists have found artefacts from prehistoric settlements here."

Hana loved that Drago knew about the history of the island.

"One legend says fairies lived here," Gal chimed in.

"That's true. They apparently flooded the area," Drago said.

"Why?" Hana asked.

"This was a beautiful green valley," Gal explained. "The local fairies lived where the island now is. Local sheep farmers were letting their sheep graze in the area, but the fairies asked them to keep the sheep from their sacred spot. The farmers ignored the fairies, which angered the fairy people so much that they flooded the area, turning it into a lake."

"Don't mess with fairies," Mae said.

"You look like a fairy," Gal said.

"Don't mess with me," Mae joked.

"Oh, I won't," Gal said.

Hana watched the two tease each other and wondered if anything was happening between them. They got on really well. They were way more relaxed with each other than her and Drago were yet. There was something about them that she couldn't quite put her finger on. She made a mental note to grill Mae about Gal later.

Mae eased the rowboat up to the pier and Gal jumped out and tied the boat securely, then helped the others step out.

Hana and Mae stood side by side, staring upwards. To get to the church and the main part of the island, they'd have to climb.

"I wouldn't've rowed if I'd known I'd have to climb a thousand stairs."

"It's ninety-nine stairs," Gal said.

"I still would've saved my energy."

Drago stood next to Hana. She felt the pressure of his hand on the base of her back. "There's another legend. Any man that carries his bride up there to marry her will have a long and happy marriage."

Hana didn't know what to say. Normally this would be a fun piece of information about this strange place, but right now, standing next to Drago, wishing he'd kiss her again, this little legend made her a bit breathless.

Gal suddenly grabbed hold of Mae, easily tossed her over his shoulder and started running up the stairs.

"This doesn't mean I'm marrying you," she squealed.

Gal thought that was hilarious. “I’m doing the modern version, where we’re just friends for life.”

Drago and Hana burst out laughing.

He turned to her, eyes sparkling. “I’m with him.” And he picked Hana up and followed Gal up the stairs. Hana watched as the boat got smaller and laughed even more as Drago began to pant and slow down.

“You’re heavy,” he wheezed.

Hana’s stomach hurt from laughing. “You’re just really unfit.”

They reached the top and Drago planted her back on the ground. Gal was lying on the pavement, pretending to be in agony.

“The fairy is so heavy,” he said.

Mae kicked him with her foot. “Get up, you wuss.”

Gal dragged himself off the ground and dusted himself off. Hana noticed the others in the distance near the church, so they made their way over to join them. Everyone was in high spirits. It was a beautiful afternoon, and the island was a picturesque oasis of calm.

The church had a steady flow of visitors making their way through it and the gang joined the queue. There was a painted fresco along one wall, and a gold altar at the end.

Hana gazed at the mural before realising what it depicted. “Oh my god.”

“God won’t help him there,” Mae quipped.

“Yes, the circumcision of Christ.” The look on Drago’s face said it all. “It’s very rare.”

“Well it can only be done once,” Mae said.

Hana laughed. “Ouch.” She noticed the others milling around a bell rope near the altar.

“That’s a wishing bell,” Drago explained.

One by one the girls pulled on the rope, eyes closed, sending their wishes out to whoever was listening. Hana's turn came and she held the rope in her hands for a moment, considering what she should ask for. What she really wanted.

She came up blank.

Other thoughts followed. To get into uni? To resolve things with Ronin and her parents? To return to Paris and have the experience she'd always wanted?

She turned and locked eyes with Drago. He was smiling and gave her a nod.

"Go on, make a wish."

Hana shut her eyes and pulled the bell.

I feel like in this moment I have everything I've ever and never dreamt about, so thank you. I leave my future in your hands, to take me where I need to go.

The bell rang out above her.

CHAPTER

# Thirty-One

The temperature had dropped by the time they boarded their boats back to the mainland. Dark clouds were gathering above the castle, creating an ominous effect.

"It looks like it's going to storm," Hana said.

"It might snow," Drago said.

Mae pointed at a beautiful villa in the distance. "Is that a hotel?"

"It is now," Drago said. "It was Tito's summer residence."

Hana had no idea who Tito was, but Mae being Mae obviously did.

"The dictator?"

"That is one opinion, and usually the American opinion."

"Who was Tito?" Hana asked.

"Slovenia used to be a part of Yugoslavia and Tito was the leader. Western governments branded him a dictator, but it's never black and white. There were certainly atrocities under him, but many Slovenians fondly remember his leadership and their quality of life under his rule."

Hana was completely confused. She'd never really considered world politics before. She noticed Mae was nodding, as if she understood, or at least was interested, so Hana gave a nod too and turned to watch the storm clouds roll in.

This time Gal rowed and they reached the shore just ahead of the others, then helped Ivan pull the boats into the shed.

They made their way back around the path towards the

house. Just as they left the public walkway and headed into the trees, a crack of thunder sounded above them.

Ada screamed and then laughed while grabbing Dina's hand. The air had turned to ice.

The sky rumbled some more, and the group all quickened their pace towards the house, reaching the garden just as a swirl of large icy drops began to fall. The sky had darkened and they all ran for the door. Drago hit the light switches as they entered the house.

Nothing.

He rushed from the room and Hana could hear him hitting switches as he went. But the house darkened again as the storm moved directly overhead.

Another crack of thunder.

"This is going to be an interesting night," Frankie said.

"Are you girls afraid of the dark?" Bor asked.

"Wasn't before now," Dina said, only half joking.

Drago appeared again, now just a shadowy figure at the door. "Okay, plan B. I'm going to start up the fire in the living room, which will give us both warmth and light."

"We'll freeze without power," Ada said.

"We have central heating that's different to our power source. So we're fine. There are some candles there, so let's use them to go and get changed into something warm, and then we'll meet back here for dinner.

"How will we cook if there's no power?" Ada's voice was shaky.

Drago gave her a very serious look. "We'll order pizza."

That broke the tension and everyone laughed. They weren't in a horror film or stuck in a house in the middle of nowhere. Town was nearby and they could have food delivered. Very civilised.

They followed Drago into the living room, where he quickly stoked the embers in the fireplace into roaring flames that lit and warmed the whole room. He grabbed some candles from the sideboard, lit them and passed them around. The girls then made their way up the stairs to get changed.

Drago appeared at Hana's side. "I'll come with you to protect you."

Hana rolled her eyes. "I'm perfectly capable of looking after myself."

"Don't you get scared?"

"No."

"I do… will you protect me?"

Hana laughed. "Come on, scaredy cat." They made their way along the darkened corridor and to Hana's room. "You wait here while I get changed."

Drago did as he was told, on demon watch at the doorway. Hana threw on track pants and layered sweaters, grabbed her wrap, and joined him again.

"Miss me?" she whispered.

He placed the candle on a nearby sideboard and drew her in, his lips grazing her ear. "I did." And their lips touched, again and again. He drew her closer, until she wasn't quite sure where she ended and he began. Her arms slid around his neck holding him close, holding herself up. She didn't need all the layers she'd put on. A fierce heat filled her. It was like nothing she'd ever experienced. If he'd asked her in that moment to return into the bedroom with him, she'd have gone. She would've agreed to anything.

But he didn't. Ever the gentleman, he pulled himself back, flustered, but maintaining control.

"I'm so tempted to..."

"Why don't we?" she said, breathless.

He took one deep breath and calmed himself before responding. "Because I know the dragons' tails would have waved for you, and so, when it happens, it needs to be perfect. Not rushed."

She rolled her eyes. "Is it that obvious?"

"Not obvious. But getting to know you... I assume."

"You're right."

He leant forward and kissed her on the forehead. "I'm really enjoying spending this time with you. If it leads to that, then I want it to be perfect for you. No regrets."

"I don't think I'd ever regret any time I spend with you, Drago." It was the truth.

He picked up the candle in one hand and slipped his fingers through hers with the other, leading her back down the halls to the stairs and the lounge below. The others were all there in various states of dress: pyjamas, tracksuits, wrapped in blankets.

"You were slow so we ordered pizza," Bor said

"Now we're telling ghost stories," Mae said.

Ada hit her with a pillow.

Hana and Drago curled up together on one of the lounges.

"I'm happy to hear some ghost stories," Hana said, ignoring Ada's glare. She liked ghost stories. "It's the perfect night for it."

"I thought you don't believe in ghosts?" Drago said.

"That's why I'm happy to hear about them."

"I guess we've already learnt about dragons," Ada said.

"And the Lake Bled fairies," Mae said.

"Yes, Bor told us about them," Frankie said.

"Do you have myths in Australia?" Drago asked.

"Of course. Australia is home to the oldest surviving

civilisation on earth," Mae said. "Australia's Aboriginal people have countless myths and legends."

"What's their main one?" Gal asked.

"That's a complicated question to answer," Mae said. "That's like asking what the main myth in Europe is. It might be one landmass, but it's home to many different languages and cultures. Australia is the same. There are many different Aboriginal nations in Australia."

"I didn't know that," said Gal.

"To be fair, lots of Australians don't either."

"So, what's one story that you know?"

"Well, Australia has a mythical creature called the Yowie."

"The what?"

The other girls brightened in a collective effort to scare the boys.

"Oh, the Yowie is terrifying," said Ada, her gorgeous eyes wide with pretend fear.

Bor looked quite concerned.

Dina took over telling the story. "The Yowie is a large, hairy creature that looks a bit like a huge man or ape. You have to be very careful when you go camping that you're not in Yowie country."

"What would it do to you?" Bor asked, glancing at Ada.

"It's difficult to say," Ada said quietly. "Mainly because no one attacked by a Yowie has ever lived to describe it."

"So, they still exist?"

"Yowies are still spotted now and then," Frankie said. "We have another terrifying creature in Australia. But this one is no myth… it's real." She paused for dramatic effect. "The drop bear."

"Oh god yes, drop bears." Hana held a hand to her chest. "I

don't want to think about them."

Frankie threw her a conspiratorial wink and Hana's heart leapt. It was the first connected moment between the two friends in days. It made Hana realise how desperately she wanted to fix the rift in their friendship.

Bor interrupted, clearly wanting to outdo the Aussies. "That's nothing. We not only have dragons and fairies, but we have a lot of ghosts."

"Everywhere has ghosts," Mae said.

"Not like ours."

Gal nodded. "It's true. Our ghosts have been dripping blood and terror for centuries, wandering the halls of our castles."

Mae chuckled. "Australia is home to the oldest continuous culture on Earth. We might not have castles but I'm pretty sure we have ghosts older than yours."

"My mum says she saw a ghost once," Ada said.

"I once went to a house in Sydney that apparently had the ghost of a woman who had been murdered there," Frankie said.

"Some people say this house is haunted," Drago said.

A massive crack of thunder sounded overhead.

"You're not serious," Hana said.

"Thought ghosts don't scare you?"

"Doesn't mean I want to actually meet one."

"So, this house is haunted?" Ada's voice wavered.

Drago nodded. "Apparently so."

"Who's the ghost?" Dina asked.

"I've never seen her but my father swears he has. Some old woman," Drago whispered. "Some say she fell from a window. But my father says she jumped. She was spurned by a lover and so she threw herself out the window but now wanders the halls looking for him."

Another blast of thunder and, despite the warm room, Hana shivered.

Drago shrugged. "Occasionally you hear a whisper… or footsteps."

A door creaked in the entrance. Everyone froze and Hana's blood turned to ice.

"I think we've had enough ghost stories," Ada whispered.

Bor looked equally terrified and wrapped a protective arm around her. Hana was unsure whether he was protecting Ada or himself.

Were those footsteps?

"Oh my god…" said Ada, her voice barely heard.

A flash of lightning drenched the room in light and Hana realised with pure horror that the ghost of the old woman was standing in the doorway.

CHAPTER

# Thirty-Two

Everyone was screaming.

Ada burst into tears.

Gal had dive bombed on top of Mae, as if protecting her.

And, in the midst of all this mayhem, Hana saw Drago jump up off the lounge, make his way over to the ghost and embrace her.

One by one the others realised that perhaps the ghost was a real person.

Bor looked embarrassed, walked over to her and gave her a hug himself.

The ghost looked amused.

Drago turned to the girls. "Everyone, please meet my grandmother Marija."

The hysteria stopped in its tracks.

His grandmother.

Frankie glanced at Hana. "Not a ghost."

"I think she's alive."

Frankie and Hana giggled at Hana's joke.

The girls stood to greet Marija. Unlike Drago's mother, his grandmother gave Hana a warm welcome, dismissing her outstretched hand and pulling her in for a hug.

"I must apologise for frightening you all," she said.

The girls all lied and assured her that she hadn't.

"Why are you all sitting in the dark?" She asked.

Drago answered her in Slovenian. She shook her head and

turned to the girls. "My grandson is not so bright. He thought there is a blackout but it's just one switch has turned off." She grabbed a candle, "Bor, come with me to the powerbox. I'll show you how this is done. I think you are more sensible than Drago."

They disappeared from the room and Drago turned to the girls, a huge grin on his face. "That was fun."

"I almost peed myself," Mae said.

"I think Bor did," Ada joked.

"So, this is your grandmother's house?" Hana asked.

"Yes, but she now lives most of the time in an apartment in the city. She'd rather be here. She loves this house, but my father insists."

Moments later, various lights around the house switched on.

Drago looked a little embarrassed. "I did think it was a blackout."

"I'm confused," Hana said. "You said you were showing us your hotel?"

"My hotel site. One day I will turn this house into the most beautiful hotel in Slovenia. Perhaps the whole of Europe."

"He's waiting for me to die." Marija appeared again.

"That's not true, Babica. Just give me the house while you're still alive. Win win."

She laughed. It was clearly a running joke between them. "One day, my dear boy, this is yours. But I'm not quite ready to give it up yet." She looked at Hana to explain. "This house has been in our family for three hundred years. I grew up here. It's a part of me."

"I'll call it Hotel Marija, in your memory," Drago teased, giving his grandmother a kiss on the top of her head.

Hana realised how small Marija was. She'd missed that

because she appeared to have such a large presence. But she was actually petite, with pale skin, and dark grey hair pulled back in a bun at the nape of her neck. She was dressed in simple navy slacks and a grey cashmere turtleneck sweater. She wore pearl earrings, and, Hana noticed, a wedding ring. She was elegant and beautiful.

"To what do we owe this surprise, Babica?"

"Danny came to visit me for afternoon tea and mentioned that he was driving up to see you. So, I decided to come too."

Drago's face lit up. "You came with Danny? Where is he?"

"He was just making a call in the car."

Now Hana was really confused. "Who's Danny?"

"He's a friend from boarding school. I was only talking to him yesterday. He was in London… and made no mention of visiting. What a surprise.

"Such a surprise," Marija agreed.

Hana watched Marija smile at her grandson. Something was up, but she couldn't put her finger on it. She shook the feeling off. What would she know; she'd only just met his grandmother.

Frankie joined the circle. "Is someone else joining us?"

"Yes, my friend Danny."

"This is quite the slumber party." Frankie turned to the girls and, in a stage whisper, said, "I hope he's hot."

Frankie laughed at her own joke and then Hana watched as her eyes widened. Anything else she was going to say was silenced. Hana followed Frankie's gaze and realised someone else had entered the room.

That someone was extremely tall, with broad shoulders, and dirty blonde hair.

"Everyone, this is my dear friend Danny."

CHAPTER

# Thirty-Three

"So everyone at school would call me Count Dracula. It was Danny who would correct them—that Dracula is from Romania and that he'd need to cross at least two country borders to get to Slovenia."

Everyone was seated around the dining room table. Large portraits of men and women Hana assumed were Drago's ancestors peered down from the ornately wallpapered walls. Despite the formal feel to the room and the mahogany dining table, there were now empty pizza boxes and beer bottles strewn around and a relaxed feel to the place.

"Were you a geography geek or something?" Mae said to Danny.

"My family owns a travel company, so I'd travelled a lot growing up."

"So did Frankie." Hana spoke for her friend, who had been rendered mute since laying eyes on Danny.

"Is that so?" Danny said to Frankie. "Why did you travel?"

"My parents decided to worldschool me and my two brothers from when we were very young."

"Worldschool? I've read about that. No formal schooling but instead a type of homeschooling where kids learn from the world around them, yeah?"

Frankie nodded. "Yep, a bit weird but I enjoyed it."

"Not weird at all. It's awesome."

Hana could see Frankie blush from the other end of the table.

Frankie was the most easy going, confident person she knew, so this was completely out of character.

"I eventually went to school, in year 10. That's where I met my friends."

"Well, I wasn't that lucky," Danny said. "We're from London but my parents sent me to boarding school, and we only travelled during vacations. And always for my parents' work."

"Danny's parents own Green Step Travel," Drago explained.

"Wow, that's a huge company," Hana said.

Danny shrugged.

"Do you work there?"

"I've branched off on my own. I'm actually launching a backpacker and young travel brand that will hopefully one day merge with the company."

"I thought it was more eco-travel?" Hana said.

"It is, but I've just launched a more youth-oriented division. It will still be eco-focused."

Marija entered the room holding a cake. "I couldn't help myself. We couldn't have pizza without cake afterwards."

"Did you just bake that?" Ada asked. "I would've helped. I love baking."

"Well there's another one in the oven if you'd like to grab that."

Ada beamed and stood, pushing her chair back and collecting a few plates to take with her. Hana watched with interest as Danny's eyes drifted over Ada. Ada didn't notice. She rarely did. But most men noticed her. Drago hadn't leered at her once, which impressed Hana. She understood why guys stared at Ada. She was exquisite. A knockout. But Danny's gaze now, matched with the one Frankie was giving him, signalled an awkward time ahead if they weren't careful.

Danny turned his attention back to Frankie. "Tell me more about your travels."

Hana felt Drago's hand slide along her thigh under the table. They locked eyes and she smiled.

"Having fun?" he asked.

"I am. A lot of fun." It was true, she was. But there were also a couple of things worrying her. She felt like Drago failed to mention some key things. Perhaps it was a cultural thing. He came across as trustworthy and honest. But those types can make the best liars. Still, in her gut she trusted him. Perhaps it was just an oversight. Three times. She certainly didn't want to make a scene right now, but she did intend to ask him to clarify everything.

"Can we go somewhere and talk?"

"Sure," he said. "I've been wanting to give you a tour of the house anyway."

Drago took Hana's hand and they left the table.

"Where are you two going?" Mae called after them.

"Tour of the house," Drago said. "We'll be back for cake."

They walked through the dining room and kitchen towards the stairs. There was also a section of the house that had been converted into a self-contained apartment where Marija appeared to live. Beyond that was a lovely sitting room and an impressive library, with floor to ceiling shelves, moving ladders, and a number of lounges, including a pair of mahogany and leather library chairs.

"Mae needs to see this," Hana said. "She'll geek out. Total book nerd."

"She's very smart," Drago said.

"Yes, she is. What do you think is going on between her and Gal?"

"Just friends." Drago seemed certain.

"They've really connected," Hana said.

"They have. As friends." The certainty with which Drago said it unnerved Hana, as if he was privy to information she wasn't.

"She's never had a boyfriend before," Hana continued.

Drago stopped and looked at Hana, as if he was about to say something. But then turned and pointed to a door. "That leads to a cellar, which I'll turn into a wine cellar. At the moment it's filled with family junk."

Hana was thrown by the sharp change of subject. Had she made some cultural faux pas? Or did he just not gossip about friends?

They climbed the stairs to the first floor, where the girls were staying. "You've seen these rooms, four of them each with their own bathroom and balcony. Your room and the room next to you has an amazing view of the lake, Julian Alps and the Karavanke. It's like the trifecta of stunning views. People will pay top dollar for that."

They moved to the next floor, with Drago speaking continuously. "The villa is built over four floors. There is a huge balcony at the rear that overlooks the forest, and any rooms at the front have a view of the lake. There is also a three-bedroom cottage on the grounds, but that's unliveable at the moment."

They mounted the next set of stairs. The house definitely got colder the higher they went. It was clear the top floors weren't lived in anymore. But Hana could totally understand why Drago loved the house so much. It was a grand home with parquet floors, marble fireplaces, high ceilings and large rooms with original features.

"What do you think?" Drago asked as they wandered the

top floor.

"It's an amazing house. It would be an incredible hotel."

"I knew you'd get it," he said, squeezing her hand.

"Does your grandmother support your plan?"

"Yes. It was her idea. My father has no real attachment to the house, but my grandmother and I both love it. She's afraid he'll sell it, so turning it into one of the company hotels, more specifically, my hotel, well that ensures it will be safe and remain in the family."

"How can he not be attached to this house?"

"My father has no time for history or nostalgia. He is focused on business. Both my parents are."

Hana took a deep breath. "Which brings me to something I've been wanting to ask."

Drago watched her, waiting for her to continue.

"How did your mother know who Frankie was?"

Drago looked confused. He clearly had no idea what she was talking about.

"When you introduced us at the party, she brushed me off, but told Frankie she loved her Instagram account."

Now the dawning occurred. He got it.

"Did you ask us to Slovenia just so Frankie would post stuff about the hotel?"

He looked horrified at the suggestion. "No, of course not."

Hana breathed a sigh of relief. She had been so worked up for no reason.

"I just told her that you should come for that reason," Drago continued.

Hana froze. Had he just admitted it? She took a step back away from him.

"Are you upset?" He clearly had no idea.

"I guess I was under the impression that you invited us to Slovenia to get to know me."

"I did."

"But you just admitted you'd told your mother about Frankie."

"I didn't realise that would upset you, Hana. I couldn't really ask my mother to sign off on a private jet and hotel rooms for five girls I'd just met, all because I thought one of them was beautiful."

Hana softened slightly and let him continue.

"I also couldn't tell her how I saw your disappointment over Paris and the hotel and wanted to do something to make a girl I barely knew happy."

More softening. At this rate she'd be a marshmallow within minutes.

"So, I told my mother what had happened to you all, and that Frankie was an important social media influencer and that I didn't want her posting stuff about the hotel fire. Mum was totally onboard with me offering you all this trip, to smooth over any possible bad press. My mother is a business woman, not a romantic."

Hana stared at him. As weird as it was, it made sense. Of course he couldn't just put five strangers on a business tab. She got that. This had been a practical way around that.

"How did you know that Frankie was an influencer? You didn't get our passports until after you'd asked us to Slovenia."

Drago raised an eyebrow. "You would make a good detective. Frankie came to the front counter while I was there and was trying to use her Instagram to talk Madame Bouchard into letting her use the private Wi-Fi. Plus, I would be blind to not notice her taking all those photos during the fire. She's very… attached to her phone."

Hana nodded. She could see he was trying to be diplomatic. He reached for her and drew her in.

"I'm so sorry that you were worried. You should have said something sooner." He nuzzled her neck. "Promise me, you'll not keep things to yourself like that. Just ask."

"I promise." She wasn't finished yet. "Why didn't you tell me you were bringing me to your grandmother's house? You called it your hotel."

Drago tilted his head to one side, soaking her in. "I always call it my hotel. Even with my grandmother. I didn't think…"

Hana nodded. He didn't think. She had a brother. She knew boys well enough to accept that. So, her final question.

"Why didn't you tell me Danny was coming?"

"Because I didn't know."

Hana raised an eyebrow. "Really?"

"I really didn't expect it. I was only in touch with him yesterday. He was in London but he didn't mention coming here at all. I guess he wanted to surprise me."

"Did you tell him about us?"

"Of course I did. I told him all about how I'd met you. I even told him that perhaps he should meet you all when you visit London." Drago gave her a hug. "Have you finished interrogating me? Shall we go and have cake?"

Hana gave a nod and they headed back down the stairs.

Drago looked over his shoulder at her. "You do trust me, don't you?"

"I do." She didn't mention that there was one person she didn't trust.

CHAPTER

# Thirty-Four

"Hana, wake up."

Hana jolted upright before her eyes had even opened, and only then did she realise it was still dark.

"Who's there?"

"It's Frankie."

"Is it a fire?"

"No, silly, it's a surprise. Get dressed, we're all meeting downstairs."

"It's still night."

"We're watching the sunrise somewhere special."

Hana switched on the bedside lamp and dragged herself out of bed. "Once… but let's not make a habit of this."

Frankie looked dishevelled, like she hadn't slept, but she had a mysterious glow to her. "Don't worry, I'm not a fan of early mornings either. C'mon, the others are awake."

Frankie disappeared out the door and Hana got dressed, washed her face, cleaned her teeth and followed her a few minutes later. Everyone was milling around at the bottom of the stairs, most looking as confused as she felt.

Danny was the first to speak. "Now that we're all here, I'm sorry I didn't give you a heads up about this, but I wasn't sure we'd get the booking until a late-night text came through. Frankie and I were the only ones still awake…"

Hana noticed Frankie and Danny exchange a look.

"Anyway, she assured me that you'd be okay being woken for

this," Danny said.

"For what?" Ada looked a little reluctant to commit to whatever plans they'd made for everyone.

Frankie jumped up and down and clapped her hands. It was more energy than anyone should display pre-sunrise. "We're going hot air ballooning over the lake."

There was a moment of collective surprise and then everyone reacted. Mae and Gal turned to each other and high-fived. Dina laughed and nodded. She seemed okay with it. Hana glanced at Ada. She looked pale.

"You guys go. I'm not going to."

Danny looked more gutted than anyone else. "You have to come. It'll be fun."

"Not for me," Ada insisted. "I'm happy to stay here."

"Don't be a downer. Come and try it."

Ada glared at him. "I said no."

Hana moved closer to Ada. "I'll stay with you."

"Actually, I'm happy to stay," Bor said from the back of the group.

Ada brushed him off. "I don't need to be babysat, Bor."

"But I do." He looked embarrassed. "I'm very scared of heights. There's no way I can go up in a balloon."

"It's true," Gal said. "He cries on a second-floor balcony."

"I can't climb ladders."

"It's why he's not tall… He stopped growing because he hates heights."

Ada laughed. "Okay, we'll stay here and I'll cook you breakfast."

"Thank you. I'd like that," Bor said, clearly relieved.

Danny looked annoyed but put on a cheery front. "Okay, you two will miss out, but everyone else is good to go?"

Drago looked at Hana. "Are you okay?"

Hana nodded. She'd always wanted to try hot air ballooning, so was actually excited about it. She was a little conflicted that Danny had organised it. Even this surprise didn't help her warm to him, but perhaps that would change by doing this together. It was an amazing thing for them all to share.

The girls gave Ada and Bor a hug and headed out to the van. Their breath turned to vapour in the icy morning air. Drago pumped the heater up in the van and waited for the windscreen to de-ice before heading off, the silence broken by the tires across the gravel.

They drove for a short time on empty dark roads before pulling into an open field. There were already a couple of cars there, their headlights shining on what Hana realised was a deflated balloon.

"This is the launch site," Danny said.

They parked and everyone got out of the car and walked over to a couple of men who were dealing with the large, colourful cloth that lay across the field, slowly filling it with hot air. The frozen grass crunched under their feet. All around them a thick mist hung in the air.

Danny greeted the men and introduced Grega, Zoran and Franc to everyone. "Grega is a very experienced pilot and will be taking us up today."

"It is a good day to fly," Grega said, and then grinned. "Every day is a good day to fly."

Hana gave him the once over and decided he looked trustworthy enough to fly her balloon. She had no idea what her subconscious checklist was to come to that conclusion. He was neat. Didn't seem drunk. Looked intelligent and serious. It's what she looked for in any pilot as she boarded a plane.

The men turned on the burner and flames blasted up into the balloon. Hana watched in amazement as it filled. The men began to lift both the balloon and the basket, which was lying on its side, until both were upright and the balloon was hovering above the basket. She turned to share her excitement with Frankie, but realised Danny had pulled her to one side and was clicking away taking photos of her. Frankie was laughing and playing up to the camera for him, but even more disturbing was the jacket she was wearing.

Fur?

Perhaps fake but she didn't think so. Hana had an eye for these things. Where the hell did she get that? It wasn't Frankie's, that's for sure.

Hana turned away.

Light started to fill the sky and Grega gathered them all around the basket.

"Please, everyone, you may climb in."

The gang didn't need to be asked twice and started climbing aboard.

"Do I need to wear a life jacket or something?" Dina joked.

"Or a parachute?" Mae added.

Everyone was excited. Hana found herself nestled in Drago's arms, in the corner of the basket. Beside her was Mae and Gal. The basket wasn't very big, so they were all pressed against each other. She looked upward at her view: the colourful, incredible inside of the balloon. Hana could feel her heart racing, but wrapped in Drago's embrace she also felt safe and excited.

Grega adjusted the furnace and the basket lurched. Within seconds they'd lifted into the sky and the ground dropped below them. The morning light rose with them and in the distance Hana could see the majestic snow-covered alps. She didn't dare look down just yet, and kept her eyes glued to the magnificent horizon.

"Look," Drago whispered in her ear.

And so she did. Because she trusted him. And she moved her gaze from the distance to up, down and all around. It was incredible. They floated over the world, the town, the forest below, and the castle watching them from its cliff perch. Bled Island called them from the lake below, as they hovered around its edges.

"Thank you for organising this, Danny," Frankie gushed and everyone else loudly agreed.

Even Hana.

The view of Lake Bled from above was astounding and, while the air was icy cold, the heat from the balloon furnace offered some warmth.

Drago's lips pressed against her ear. "I'm so happy I get to experience this with you."

"Me too," she whispered.

They drifted through time and space for what could have been hours or minutes.

"It's not at all frightening," Dina said.

"Ada still wouldn't've coped," Mae said.

"Same with Bor," Gal added.

"Pity," Danny said. "I really thought Ada would've enjoyed this."

Hana's eyes narrowed as she watched him. Why did he have to go ruin her warm and fuzzy feeling of gratitude towards him? How would he know what Ada, or any of them, enjoyed? He didn't know them. And she didn't trust him. She didn't know why, and, really, she had him to thank for this amazing experience… but something wasn't sitting right for Hana. And it wasn't just the way his hand was stroking Frankie. There was an intimacy there that suggested something had happened between them, and yet it was blatantly obvious that he was more interested in Ada.

Hana turned away. She wouldn't let her suspicions about him ruin this magical morning.

All too soon, Grega was speaking to his ground crew via a radio, and then easing the balloon in the direction of a suitable landing spot. The landing itself was a little rough, with the basket bumping along the field, before being caught and roped down by the ground crew who'd driven there. Grega opened a valve and the air escaped, bringing the enormous balloon to rest.

They disembarked from the basket and everyone hugged each other in excitement. One by one the girls hugged Danny and thanked him for organising the experience. Hana was last. She tried to make it quick, but he pulled her in just a little too tight and for a little too long. She stiffened, stepping back with a tight smile.

"How much do we owe you, Danny?" Hana pulled her wallet from her bag.

"Oh no, that flight is on me."

"Oh no, there's no way we'll allow you to pay for all of us."

He shrugged. "What are friends for?"

"Friendship?" Hana suggested.

"Well, I'm hoping my shout this morning will fast-track that." And, with a wink, he turned and walked off towards Frankie, who he'd clearly fast-tracked something with.

CHAPTER

# Thirty-Five

They were back at Camp Dracula and decided to take it easy for the rest of the day. Drago, Bor and Gal dropped the girls off and then headed into town to pick up some traditional desserts that they swore everyone needed after the balloon flight. Hana was napping, curled up on the lounge with Mae, while Dina and Ada were reading across from them. The fire crackled and every time Hana closed her eyes, she drifted into a relaxed sleep filled with flashes of Drago and the feeling that she was still floating over Bled.

"Guys, we need to talk," Frankie's voice brought her back to reality. Hana opened her eyes and saw her in the doorway. She entered and sat next to Ada and waited until she had everyone's attention.

"I've had an offer. We've had an offer."

Hana sat up and watched as Frankie appeared to calm herself. Why was she wound up?

"I know that our itinerary has altered a bit over the past few days. Well… there's an offer to alter it some more. For a week."

"Not following," Mae said simply, summing up how everyone felt.

"I've been offered an all-expenses tour. I said I'd only do it if you could all come."

Mae's eyes widened. "For free?"

"For free. Tour bus and guide, hotel rooms and all sights." Frankie was obviously excited and rightly so. It was a major coup for her as an influencer.

Dina, Ada and Mae immediately showed their support.

"That's incredible."

"Congratulations."

"How would this work if we did it?"

"The tour starts next week. We'd join it in Prague and finish up a week later in Budapest." Frankie clearly wanted to do this and was trying to enthuse the others. "But we're going to Italy," Hana reminded them.

"Things change," Dina said, attempting to keep things in balance. "Look at the trip so far. Lots of things have changed."

Hana didn't respond. Dina was right. Which annoyed her.

"It's a free trip, Hana," Frankie said, as if Hana might've missed that info before.

"What about Italy?"

Frankie was clearly getting frustrated. "I don't know. We can fit it in somewhere. Or miss it. This is a great opportunity."

"Who offered it to you?"

Frankie looked embarrassed. "Danny. He has started his own travel company called Grassroots Travel. Tours for the under thirty market. He's invested in a small fleet of buses, mapped out the tours and it launches…"

"Don't tell me, next week." Hana said.

"Yes, next week," Frankie said. "I haven't said anything to you all about this yet, but I really like him. And I think he likes me."

Hana glanced at Ada, who was staring down at her nails. She gets it, thought Hana.

"We've spent some time together and he's so amazing. I've never met anyone like him before."

Lucky, thought Hana.

"And he feels it's like fate that we met and can complement each other's businesses," Frankie gushed.

"Last time I looked you had almost half a million followers, and he's yet to launch. So he gains more from this than you do."

"Well we get a free trip," Frankie shrugged. "And remember, we came here for you."

This really annoyed Hana. "Do you mean Slovenia, which I was outvoted on, because you all wanted to take Drago's offer up?"

"Yes, but look how it's worked out for you."

Hana was furious. Yes it had worked out well, but that didn't mean that the moment she was outvoted on her dream destination hadn't happened. It had.

"This still isn't what I wanted. I wanted to be in Paris, in a beautiful hotel, visiting galleries and falling in love with some French guy and instead I ended up in Slovenia because I was outvoted by my supposed friends."

"I'm really sorry that it worked out so badly for you," came a deep voice from the door.

Hana turned, mortified, to see Drago standing in the doorway, and Bor and Gal trying to hide out of sheer embarrassment behind him.

Hana jumped up and ran to him but he lurched back.

"That's not what I meant, Drago."

"Perhaps my English isn't that great, because my interpretation of it was that everything that has happened between us, and in my country, is nothing but a mistake, because it's not Paris."

"It's just Paris was a dream that went bad, but this is so much better."

Drago gave her a look of disdain. "Save it for your French

boyfriend, Hana." And with that he turned and strode out the door.

Hana looked at Bor and Gal in despair. They seemed to take pity on her.

"We brought cake," Bor said.

Hana burst into tears and bolted up the stairs.

CHAPTER

# Thirty-Six

"What is your problem?" Frankie burst into Hana's room. "Or more to the point, what is your problem with me?"

"That you don't know just goes to show how self-absorbed you are right now."

"You know what? I'm not psychic, and you're really bloody good at covering stuff up. What I am sure of is the tension between us. The feeling of walking on eggshells around you all the time. Beyond that, I have no idea why you're angry with me. But I'm over it."

Hana lifted her head from her tear-stained pillow. "How awful for something in your life to not be Instagram worthy."

"Right, so it is that. My Instagram?"

"I thought I'd made it obvious."

"No, you didn't. You sent really mixed messages, judging me one minute and then taking a free cocktail dress the next."

Hana felt ashamed. "Yes, that's true. But I wanted to impress Drago's parents. Not that it mattered because his mother ignored me in her stampede to get to you."

Frankie looked hurt. "That wasn't my fault."

"You still went off with her to take some snazzy photos."

"Like I had a choice? I didn't want to make a scene. I just wanted the whole night to end. I saw how upset you were. And rightly so. That stupid cow treated you like you were a nobody and I know you're special." Frankie's voice cracked. "Honestly, she was a shallow cow who should sue her surgeon. The fact that

Drago is so nice is miraculous. That's the kind of mother that normally eats her young."

Hana smiled through her tears. She couldn't help it. Frankie watched her and cracked her own smile.

"You like Drago?" Hana said quietly.

"Everyone likes Drago. He's a nice guy and he's good for you."

Hana started to sob again. "Not that it matters now. I've completely stuffed it."

"Man, you really are Japanese when it comes to confronting stuff. You just won't do it. Me, him… whatever happened with Ronin. Come on, Han, confront stuff, resolve it, move on."

Hana jumped off the bed and faced Frankie. "Fine, I'm confronting this: you don't think he brought us here to Slovenia to trade off your Instagram profile?"

"No, I don't. In fact, he's never mentioned it. His mother did, but he's never said a word about it. It's clear his focus is on you." Frankie put her hands out as if to plead. "Why do you hate my work so much? It pays for me to be here."

"I do understand that."

"And I didn't take a photo of Ada being mugged for social media. I just knew in that moment it might help the police."

"I know that too," Hana admitted.

"Then why do you have such a problem with me?"

Here goes… "You posted that awful photo of me when we arrived at the Paris hotel. You used my disappointment to garner likes, and it worked. Over 25000 of them last time I looked."

Frankie's eyes widened in shock. "Is that what started all this?"

"Well… yes. You posted that without asking permission, and it was humiliating. I was utterly humiliated."

Frankie burst into tears. "I'm so sorry. You're right, I should never've posted it without your go ahead. I just wasn't thinking. I promise not to ever do that again."

This totally disarmed Hana. Floored her. Frankie completely accepted responsibility. No 'ifs' or 'buts' or defensiveness.

She looked at her friend now, her tear-stained face. How could she continue being angry with her? And more than that, how could she tell her how she personally felt about Danny? It wasn't based on anything, just intuition, and that simply wasn't enough to break her friend's heart over.

Hana reached out and hugged Frankie. It was a warm, tight embrace of two long-lost friends.

"I'm so sorry," Frankie cried.

"I'm so sorry too," Hana sniffed.

"Will you come on the tour?"

How could she say no? Frankie was clearly struggling with feelings for Danny. Okay, she might win the two-minute noodle award for developing those feelings, but Hana knew there'd been enough hurt for one day. For one trip. She nodded. "Let's do it. All expenses paid. I'll go further off my map."

Frankie looked as though she'd won Lotto and threw her arms around Hana again.

They hugged each other tight and didn't let go.

"Promise we'll never fight again."

"Promise."

"I love you so much. You're my best friend."

It could've been either of them or both of them who said it.

# CHAPTER Thirty-Seven

After Frankie went back downstairs, Hana washed her face and steeled herself to face everyone again. She needed to apologise to a few people, but most of all to Drago. She stared at herself in the mirror. How did she mess that up so badly?

She realised her phone was ringing and ran back into her bedroom, thinking it might be Drago. It wasn't. It was Ronin, video messaging her. Part of her wanted to ignore it. She felt so good about fixing things with Frankie, but also knew it would be good to fix things with her brother too. This couldn't drag on forever. Resolution might as well be now, whichever way that went.

She pressed accept and readied herself. It was a conversation she'd dreaded having, and yet demanded from Ronin. She stared down the camera on her phone and saw that Ronin wasn't alone.

"Mum? What are you doing in Japan?"

"I'm in Sydney. Ronin is here for the weekend."

Her mother and Ronin were side by side, thousands of kilometres away, but Hana could still feel the tension. She had no idea what had happened. Had Ronin changed his mind and gone home to tell her? Had she found out herself?

Ronin began. "You were right, Han. I should have confronted this ages ago. When you first told me to."

It was a good start and Hana let her guard down slightly.

"So, I flew back here to talk to Mum… and it hasn't gone as

I expected."

Ronin smiled at their mother who smiled back. This was not at all what Hana expected either. Where were the tears? Where was her mother's heartbreak?

Her mother took over. "Darling, I wish you two had spoken to me earlier. I can't imagine what you've gone through. I could have explained things."

"Explained what?"

"I can assure you, your father is not having another affair."

Hana felt terrible, but decided to speak openly. "I know it's awful, Mum, and difficult to believe, but Dina found Midori's robe at the beach house. I think that speaks for itself."

"Your father is not having an affair with Midori."

Her mother seemed sure, but what if she was in denial?

"He's done it before," is all Hana could manage.

"I know. And when he did, he broke our trust. Not just mine, but yours and Ronin's trust as well."

Hana nodded. "He did."

"I guess I haven't been clear with you both though," her mother said. "He's earned mine back. I trust him 100 percent."

This surprised Hana. She'd simply assumed that there was an element of insecurity around their relationship.

"Now, to explain the robe, I need to also tell you another story. Your father was not my first boyfriend. In fact, he wasn't even my first Japanese boyfriend."

Whoa, talk about coming from left field. But what did this have to do with anything?

Her mother continued. "I was seventeen and had a summer romance with an exchange student called Kenji from Hiroshima who was staying with our neighbours. I guess I've always had a thing for Japanese guys."

Awkward. Hana shifted around in her seat, uncomfortable.

"It was a lovely romance, and we stayed in touch via letters, until I met your father.

When your father did have the affair a few years ago, I tracked Ken down. It wasn't hard. His family owns one of Japan's largest sake breweries, which he now runs. He was delighted to hear from me. Still as kind as he was all those years ago. He'd recently lost his wife to cancer. I figured my marriage was over. So, we decided to meet. In Hawaii."

"I remember your trip to Hawaii," Hana said quietly. "I thought you went for work."

"Well, I didn't. And I don't need to tell you why I went there. You're an adult now, Hana, and can work that out. But when Kenji and I met there, something else happened."

Hana watched her mother carefully down the phone. Ronin was sitting quietly beside her. It was clear that he'd heard this story already.

"When we arrived in Hawaii, we each found a friend. I found a man grieving very deeply for his wife, whom he loved very much. And he found me utterly heartbroken over your father. We both went there thinking we were reconnecting as childhood sweethearts, but instead we were both in desperate need of someone who could understand our pain. We spent five days talking, crying, supporting each other through the toughest times of our lives."

"As friends?"

Her mother nodded. "Friends. Nothing more."

"Why are you telling me this?"

"Because Midori is Kenji's daughter."

Hana was floored. She did not expect that.

"I don't understand."

"Kenji opened up about his daughter, Midori. He was very worried about her. She wasn't coping with her mother's death. She'd gone to an international school and went to university in Melbourne. She was working for a Japanese company in Hiroshima and struggling. She didn't fit in. Wasn't typically Japanese. Kenji was beside himself with worry."

"You gave your old boyfriend's daughter a job?"

"No, your father hired her. She's smart. Qualified. And needed to be in a more international environment."

"So Dad knows who she is?" Hana asked.

Her mother chuckled. "He suggested it. He's met Kenji. They're friends. Hana my love, the world isn't black and white; it's shades of grey and every colour in-between."

Hana had to ask. "Do you think Dad is having an affair with her?"

"Absolutely not."

"Then why was her robe at the beach house?"

Her mother glanced at Ronin who gave a nod. "She has a key and goes there sometimes… with her girlfriend. Her female partner."

"Excuse me?"

Ronin laughed and butted in. "One of the reasons Kenji was worried about his daughter in a traditional Japanese company was because she's gay. It also explains why Midori is so reserved at work. She just doesn't want anyone to know her personal business. She's used to wearing thick armour and giving nothing away."

"They can still be a bit funny about that in Japan," her mum said. "Your father and I like Midori and her girlfriend. We said they could use the beach house when they wanted."

This conversation had not gone the way Hana had expected.

She was filled with questions, and curiosity, but mostly with relief.

"It's time you and Ronin put your father's affair behind you, just like I have."

"It turned everything upside-down."

"It did. But life is like that, Hana. Sometimes you need a different view of things."

"None of us needed to go through that."

"No. But I certainly needed a reality check on how much I loved him. I don't condone the affair, but I'd given up on our marriage in other ways. The result of that time is that we're stronger and more in love than ever. Sometimes awful things happen and afterwards you're grateful for them."

"Really? Even at my age?"

Ronin grinned at his sister. "Ask Dina about that. Her world fell apart, but because of that she went to Japan and met me."

It was true. Hana knew it. She began to cry. She realised that she'd been living in a limbo, thinking her parent's marriage was meaningless, that Ronin was paying penance for selling their father's designs, and that there was always going to be another thing that tore them apart.

Instead, her family was rock solid. Her brother and her just hadn't got the memo.

"Thanks for going to Australia, Ronin."

"Thanks for telling me to."

"Usually you don't listen to me."

"Normally you talk a lot of crap, but this made sense. It just took me a while to get it."

"Dina talked to you, didn't she?"

Ronin gave her a sheepish grin. "Maybe. A little."

They laughed.

Her mother stared at her through the screen, so much love in one look. “Do you want to talk about your HSC results?”

Hana shook her head. “I’m guessing you logged on and saw them.”

“Yes. I think you did well.”

“Not well enough.”

“Darling, it won’t be long and you’ll look back and realise those numbers meant very little.”

Hana loved that her parents never put academic pressure on her. Which was good because she put enough pressure on herself.

Ronin glanced at their mother and leant forward, staring down the phone.

“Want to tell us why it looks like you’ve been crying?”

Hana felt the urge to start crying again but held back. “Boy trouble,” she mumbled.

“A nice boy?”

Hana nodded.

Her mother smiled. “Then go work it out.”

CHAPTER

# Thirty-Eight

Hana entered the living room and found the other four girls huddled around talking, as if making plans. The tour probably.

Mae jumped up and grabbed Hana by the shoulders and moved her into a chair. "We've got something to say, so sit."

"Sounds like an order," Hana said.

She did as she was told and took a moment to look around. Her friends all looked relaxed. Ada was smiling. Even Frankie looked happy to see her.

"What's going on?" Hana asked.

"We've made a group decision," Mae said.

Hana immediately bristled. "Without me here. Good one."

"Before you arc up… if you don't like this decision, we won't mind. In fact, your vote is the decider." Dina smiled.

"I agreed to go on the tour. Isn't that enough?"

The others shook their heads, mysterious smiles all round.

Mae paused for dramatic effect. "We think we should go back to Paris for a few days."

Hana was stunned. She didn't expect this and the expression on her face clearly showed it.

"We have a few days before we need to be in Prague. We have some extra money now that all the travel and accommodation on the tour is paid for. We were talking about where we should go, and Paris seems to be the obvious choice."

"But Paris was awful!" Hana finally spoke.

"It wasn't awful," Dina said. "It just wasn't what you expected.

Or what any of us expected."

"So why go back?" Hana asked. "Are we suckers for punishment?"

As soon as Hana said the words, she knew she was wrong. Paris hadn't been a punishment. It had been a learning curve. It wasn't what she expected. But her expectations had locked her into a picture of something that was impossible to match. From the moment she slapped eyes on the hotel, Paris had let her down. It had betrayed her. And that seemed to be a running theme. She felt like her father, her brother, her friends had all betrayed her. Most of all, the city of her dreams had betrayed her.

When, in fact, none of that was true.

She had done herself a huge disservice by being so black and white about everything, and when life threw her shades of grey, she couldn't handle it.

She turned to Ada. "You'd go back to Paris after what happened there?"

Ada nodded. "Drago was right. This will all make a great story one day. But more than that… it's made us all stronger. Look what we've dealt with. Being robbed, a fire, ghosts… changing plans."

"A biggie for you," Mae said.

Ada agreed. "Huge for me… changing plans so dramatically and spontaneously."

"We've also dealt with our first real fight," Frankie said.

Hana locked eyes with her friend. They were okay now, she knew that.

"We're stronger," Ada said.

"Better travellers," Mae added.

"We can do this," Dina said. "You can do this. You can go

back to Paris and see it the way you're meant to now."

Hana nodded. Her friends were right. She'd stepped so far off her rigid map that she could step back on now, no expectations, and perhaps see Paris through fresh eyes.

Not the eyes from a week ago, where nothing was as it should be.

And certainly not the imaginary eyes, from years of being sure of how it would be.

But fresh eyes, ready to experience whatever came her way.

"Let's go to Paris," she whispered.

The girls clasped hands, excited, and happy.

Paris it was.

CHAPTER

# Thirty-Nine

Hana knocked on the door of Marija's apartment.

"Come in, Hana."

Hana entered, approaching Drago's grandmother warily. "You knew it was me?"

"Of course. You're looking for Drago?"

Hana nodded.

Marija stared at her for a moment. "Sit with me for a minute."

Hana did as she was told and took a good look around the room. It was lovely, with big bay windows, cream carpet and furnishings in shades of white and peach. It had clearly been renovated in recent years and had a much more modern feel than the rest of the house.

She turned her attention back to Marija who was watching her carefully. Taking Frankie's advice onboard, she decided to broach things first. "I said some things that I didn't mean, and that were awful, and Drago has disappeared. I'm very sorry. I really don't want to hurt him."

"Oh, I believe that completely. You'll work it out with him."

This threw Hana. She was expecting the protective grandmother. Perhaps a lecture. Certainly disapproval.

"My dear, I didn't ask you to sit so I could lecture you about hurting my grandson. I think you're good for him. You're very smart."

Hana blushed. She really had no idea where this was going.

"Much smarter than him in some regards."

Okay, weird, but she'd eventually get to the point.

"I've been watching you carefully. All of you. And you are the only one who really sees through Danny." She leant forward and lowered her voice. "Don't ever trust that young man."

Hana was floored. She really didn't expect that.

"He can't be trusted."

Hana nodded.

"You can't stop your friend from getting involved, but you must be there to pick up the pieces, dear."

Another nod.

"I'm so glad you're with Drago. He's oblivious to that boy. He thinks… how do you say in English? That the moon shines out his buttocks?"

Hana giggled. "Your English is excellent."

"It's why I came to Bled with Danny. I thought I'd have to look after my grandson, but I see you're doing that."

Hana and Marija shared a conspiratorial look.

"He's in the cottage at the back of the house."

"Thank you." Hana gave Marija a hug and ran for the door.

# CHAPTER Forty

"Drago?"

The cottage door was already half open, so Hana pushed it back and entered the dark hallway. If the main house was for vampires, this place was surely a nest for zombies. It was separate from the main house, with access along an overgrown path. The small cottage was in original condition and in desperate need of work… or demolition.

"Drago, if you're here, please let me know…"

Silence.

"… because I'm actually a little creeped out."

Nothing for a moment, and then a voice. "But you don't believe in ghosts."

She followed the voice down the hall. "I don't… but the jury is still out on zombies." She entered a large living room that, thanks to two big back windows, was filled with light. High wooden beams overhead. Boxes and old furnishings piled everywhere. Three doors leading to other rooms, or perhaps the depths of hell.

And there was Drago, in an armchair reading, legs on an ottoman, beer in hand.

He waited for her to speak first, so she did.

"I'm so sorry. I didn't mean any of that."

"Yes you did."

"I was just trying to point out that I'd been outvoted on Slovenia. I wanted to stay in Paris and chase my dream, but the part you didn't wait around to hear was… how surprised I was to find my dream here." She looked up at the dilapidated cottage with rotting beams. "Not specifically here, but in Slovenia. With you."

Drago put both the book and the beer down. He was listening.

"I didn't mean that I'm still upset about them outvoting me. I'm not. How could I be when I've had this time with you. But I was really hurt at the time because they knew how I'd always wanted to go to Paris."

He stood and walked over to her. Face to face, she just wanted to reach out and draw him in, but she sensed he wasn't ready yet.

"You said you wanted a French guy."

"I admit, I did fantasise about that when I dreamt about the rest of my Paris trip. But it was stupid, an unrealistic fantasy. This is real."

"Is it?" he asked.

"It's real for me, yes. Scarily so," she admitted.

"Scarily, as in how scared of zombies you are?"

"More so."

He sighed and gave a nod. "I understand how disappointed you were about Paris."

"I thought I was at the time. I've always loved French design. I had this picture in my mind of how things should be. But really, I'm so happy none of that worked out."

Drago reached out and drew her in. She could feel his breath. "You know, meeting you wasn't my plan either. Falling for an Australian girl is so far off my map too. It's highly inconvenient, geographically."

Hana had never considered that. And then realised what else he'd said… "You're falling for me?"

"Of course. How could I not. You're perfect."

"I'm not at all, but I'm really happy you think I am." She smiled. "I'm falling for you too."

Drago beamed. "That is very good to hear."

"This is crazy. How will this work? What do we do now?"

"We'll work it out. You're going on Danny's tour, right? Perhaps we can meet afterwards."

"I'd love that," Hana said, pulling him in closer. "And the girls have just announced that they want us to return to Paris." She felt him stiffen slightly. "I know this is awkward, after what happened today, but I do want to give that city one more try. So I was thinking… you could come with us?"

Drago searched her face. "You'd really want that?"

"Well yes, you'll come in handy if there's a fire."

"Good point."

"We could ask Gal and Bor too. They're great value. I'm not ready to say goodbye to them either."

"But won't we get in the way of any French suitors?"

"Hopefully," Hana whispered. "Because I'd much prefer my Slovenian suitor, if that's okay with you."

The kiss he gave her indicated that he was more than okay with that.

CHAPTER

# Forty-One

Hana woke early after the best sleep she'd had in ages. She pulled back the curtains and let the morning sun stream in.

*Good morning, Paris!*

They had arrived at the hotel at a little before nine the evening before. This time, her room was lovely, with stone floors, whitewashed walls and wooden beams overhead. There was a large bed with an upholstered headboard and an embroidered cover in rich shades of burgundy. The room was filled with ornate touches, like the bronze patina on the light fittings and door handles, and gold-framed watercolours on the walls. The bathroom was large enough to swing a cat—albeit one with a short tail. All in all, it was perfect.

She opened the window. The sill had a wrought-iron railing that she could lean on and watch Paris below. And she did exactly that. She stuck her head out and looked down at the street, and then across at the rooms in nearby buildings. She could hear a siren in the distance—a French one. The air was icy and her breath came out in clouds. The streets of Paris beckoned her.

Drago had suggested Hotel Antoinette. It was within their budget—just—a lovely mid-range boutique hotel. Every detail was utterly perfect. The wallpaper throughout was hand-painted, and the dark wood floors were covered in oriental carpets. The whole place was an explosion of colour, with unusual fabrics and lampshades. In the foyer, a fireplace warmed the room. There were an assortment of lounge chairs and divans around small wooden tables. And scattered around the hotel, from foyer to hallways to the small café on the ground floor, were stunning flower arrangements that her grandmother would have approved of. The shades, the form and the combinations took her breath away.

As did he.

She turned now to see Drago stretched out asleep in their bed. Nothing had happened. At least that hadn't happened. They'd slept wrapped in each other's arms. She'd been nervous about sharing a room with him, but once they'd checked in it seemed like the most natural thing in the world. She had no idea if anything more would happen. She was certainly tempted, but it was Drago who whispered to her last night that they would still take their time.

They had all the time in the world, he'd said.

He stirred, rolled onto his side and opened his eyes, giving her a sleepy smile. "What a great sight to wake up to," he said.

She ran back to the bed and slipped under the covers beside him. "We're in Paris!"

"I'm glad you're happy."

"I am, but I was also happy in Slovenia. It seems to be you."

Drago kissed her forehead.

"Frankie messaged me. The others have gone down for breakfast," Hana said.

Drago grabbed her and rolled on top of her. "Good timing, otherwise I might go back on our agreement last night to wait."

"That was your idea, not mine."

He stared at her for a moment, and then dragged himself off her and out of bed with a groan. "You're killing me."

A minute later, he was in the shower.

Hana opened her case and hung her clothes in the small

closet. They were staying three nights, and then Drago, Bor and Gal would fly home, and Danny would go with the girls to Prague, where they joined his tour.

He wouldn't travel with them. Thankfully.

That had been something Ada had suggested. The girls all agreed that these few days in Paris would be fun, but then they wanted some travel time together again.

Hana dressed in jeans and a sweater. She checked herself out in the mirror. She felt completely different about Paris this time. She really didn't want that to be about Drago. She didn't want to be the type of girl whose happiness depended on a guy.

But she knew it was more than just her feelings for Drago that were making her so happy today.

She had sorted things out with Ronin. Her father wasn't having an affair. Her parents were okay. Her friendship with Frankie was back on track.

And finally, she realised that she really didn't have any expectations about Paris this time. She'd let go of them. She was thrilled that the hotel was so beautiful. That was a nice start. But really, she'd fallen in love with Slovenia, which was a lovely surprise. Anything that happened now was just a bonus.

Once Drago was dressed, they joined the others in the hotel café for the buffet breakfast. Hana poured herself a coffee and placed two pains au chocolat on her plate. She was famished. She made her way over to her friends who had joined two tables together and sat next to Drago. Noticing a display of parrot tulips and miniature roses, she leaned in close to the arrangement to get a better look. Pine needles, eucalyptus pods. What a great choice.

"Do you miss the Bouchard?" Drago whispered.

Hana gave him a cheeky grin. "I was just thinking how this

doesn't compare."

"Maybe you'll return once my family has renovated it."

Hana soaked him in. He was so handsome, in dark jeans and a black turtleneck sweater. "Maybe."

She was so content to be where she was. She didn't need to rush anywhere or make grand plans for the future. She simply was. She was going with the river.

She sat back and enjoyed watching her friends with their breakfast banter.

Mae and Gal seemed joined at the hip and yet it didn't seem romantic. Hana couldn't quite put her finger on what was going on between them, but it was interesting.

Bor, Ada and Dina were relaxed and chatting. Ada was eating a big breakfast.

Frankie and Danny were huddled together while he talked to her about the tour. Hana watched them for a moment and then decided to put her unease to one side for the day. If she'd learnt anything on this trip, it was that things would be resolved, but sometimes you just needed to be patient.

Mae tapped her glass with her knife. "Attention please! Gal thinks we should visit the Marmottan Monet museum."

"It's my favourite museum," Gal explained. "And doesn't have the crowds of the Louvre."

"Sounds good. Lining up to see the Mona Lisa has never been my thing," Danny said.

Hana hated that she agreed with him. And she loved Monet.

"The museum also has pieces by artists like Gauguin, Morisot, Pissarro, Guillaumin, Sisley and Renoir," said Gal, still selling it.

"My brother is such a weirdo," Bor chuckled.

"It's why we get on," Mae said, giving Gal a light shove on

the shoulder.

"I think Hana should decide today. After all, Paris is her thing." Frankie turned to Hana. "What's on your itinerary?"

"I don't have one," Hana said.

"But you must've before."

"Yep. But not now. I'm really happy to go with the flow." Hana smiled at Gal. "I love Monet."

"Great," Ada said, gathering up her scarf and coat. "Let's get some culture in us."

"And then we can go for beer after," Bor said.

The others all laughed and gathered up their coats.

Hana watched as Danny offered to help Ada into her coat, but Ada blanked him, put it on herself, and then headed for the exit. Danny turned back to Frankie and helped her instead. Hana wished Danny would disappear, but knew that wasn't going to happen anytime soon. They were tied into him and his travel company for the next week.

A lot could happen in a week. Of that she was certain.

Drago held Hana's jacket out and she slipped into it, giving him a shy smile. She refused to worry about Danny today.

They all made their way out of the café, through the entrance of the hotel and into the morning sunshine.

She felt Drago slip his hand around hers, and she hit the Paris pavement, surrounded by her friends, ready to see where the day took them.

## ABOUT THE AUTHOR

**Jane Tara** is a Lost Girl. She has lived in six countries and travelled extensively in-between. She lived in Japan for many years and thinks of Tokyo as her second home.

Jane has published over seventy children's books, a number of plays, and five novels. She currently lives with her two sons in Bondi Beach, Sydney, but spends part of each year travelling.

**RUA Lost Girl?**

Visit www.rualostgirl.com for updates, sneak peeks and bonus content.